Transport in Barrow in Furness

SEMPER · SURSUM.

Harry Postlethwaite

Contents

INTRODUCTION

The town of Barrow in Furness is situated at the end of the Furness Peninsula in the North West of England. Traditionally, the Furness area was part of the County of Lancashire but was separated from the main part of the County by part of the County of Westmorland, the boundary of which came to the sea at Arnside. The town was granted Municipal Borough status in 1867 and County Borough status in 1889. Under Local Government reorganisation in 1974, the Furness area was combined with the counties of Cumberland and Westmorland, together with part of the West Riding of Yorkshire to form the County of Cumbria.

The town is somewhat isolated, being situated at the end of the A590 road, sometimes described as the longest cul-de-sac in the country. It is nevertheless a substantial community with a population of around 70,000. It has long been associated with shipbuilding, particularly the building of submarines and in recent years nuclear powered submarines. It is a seaport and was the location of the headquarters of the Furness Railway Company which operated from Carnforth through Barrow to Whitehaven, with branches to Coniston and Lakeside.

On the formation of the County of Cumbria in 1974 Barrow had the only municipal transport system in the county.

In 1877 there was a horse bus service which operated from Barrow Island via the town centre to Abbey Road. This was not a financial success and public transport in the town really started with the tramway.

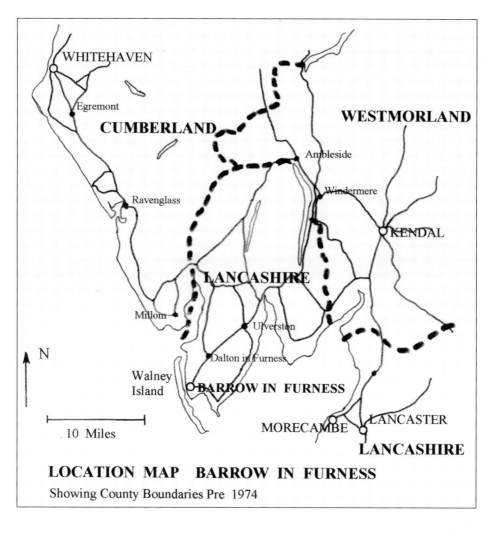

LOCATION MAP   BARROW IN FURNESS

Showing County Boundaries Pre 1974

THE TRAMS

The Barrow in Furness Corporation Act 1881 authorised the establishment of a tramway system and originally eight routes were envisaged. No action was taken until August 1883 when a special committee was formed which, in September 1883, resolved to send a deputation to inspect tramway systems at other towns. On 3rd October 1883 tramways at Middlesbrough, Stockton, Sunderland, South Shields and Tynemouth were inspected. Five days later the deputation travelled to Portrush in Northern Ireland to inspect the electric railway between Portrush and Bath Mills near the Giant's Causeway, actually travelling on the line before it was officially opened. On 10th October 1883, the tramways at Preston, Bolton, Bury, Birkenhead and Southport were visited. Their recommendation was the establishment of a steam tramway system of 4ft gauge, this gauge being preferred to 4ft 8½ins and effecting a saving estimated at £220 per single track mile. Offers were invited in October 1883, from promoters and lessees of tramway systems to make proposals for Barrow. In November 1883 a Mr Vawser of Manchester made an offer and agreement was reached with

him which resulted in a Provisional Order for the operation of tramways being approved on 27th February 1884. This was confirmed by the Tramways Order Conformation (number 3) Act of 1884 which authorised construction of the undermentioned routes. The managers were named as Robert Wilkinson and Robert McLay.

1. Abbey to Town Hall

Commencing from the Lodge Gate to Crosslands House the line was single track to the first loop on the corner west of Crosslands House. It then continued single to the Strawberry Hotel with a loop midway between Crosslands House and this point. The next loop was at the top of East Mount with another at the foot of Victoria Road and a further one at Hibbert Road. The last loop was between Rawlinson Street and Dalton Road.

A somewhat dilapidated and overloaded steam tram makes its way along Duke Street. It was reported that the steam trams were in very poor condition towards the end of their days. This view well illustrates the situation. *(GHC)*

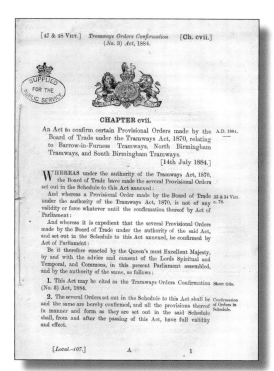

Detail from the 1884 Confirmation Act.

In Ramsden Square the line made a triangular junction with the line from the Ironworks / Steelworks. The line then continued along Duke Street to the Town Hall, being double as far as Cavendish Street with a loop opposite the old fire station at the corner of Market Street.

2. Ironworks/Steelworks to Ramsden Square

The line commenced at a triangular turning point at the junction of Walney Road and Duke Street and there was a loop between Blake Street and Anson Street before making a triangular junction with the Abbey line at Ramsden Square.

3. Roose to Town Hall

The line terminated at the east side of Roose railway station bridge and continued from there by way of a long loop over the bridge becoming single on the far side of the bridge with a loop on the next corner in Roose Road. The next loop was opposite Salthouse Villa at the junction of what became Friars Lane. There were further loops

under Salthouse Railway Bridge, beyond Marsh Street, two short loops in St George's Square and a final loop at the junction of Ramsden Street and the Strand. From this point the line was single along Duke Street to Schneider Square where it made a triangular junction with the Ramsden Dock and Abbey routes.

4. Ramsden Dock Station to Town Hall

The starting point was the forecourt of Ramsden Dock Station and a turning circle was provided in the station yard. There were loops halfway up the approach to the bridge over the Dock Branch Railway, opposite the entrance to the Harbour Office, at the end of Anchor Road on the town side of the Devonshire Hotel. It was then single to the Shipyard Gate and double across the High Level Bridge on the mainland side to where it joined the Abbey and Roose routes at the Town Hall.

Routes 6 and 7, authorised under the 1881 Act, were not constructed. The former was to have operated from the junction with Tramway 3 opposite Rawlinson Street and operating along that street to a junction with Tramway 5 on Salthouse Road. Tramway 7 would have commenced with a junction with Tramway 6 and thence operated along Ramsden Street to terminate in a proposed Corporation store yard. These routes were significantly different to the original 1881 Act authorisations. The route from the Steelworks to St Georges Square was totally abandoned, this being the principal difference along with other minor changes.

Formal notice was given by the tramway company on 25th April 1884 of its intention to commence work and in June 1884 the contractor, Mr Fell, stated that he was commencing with the work of laying the tracks and that the work would be overseen for the Corporation by the Borough Engineer. Work continued and track laying was completed in June 1885 by which time engines had arrived and were tested on various sections of the track in readiness for the Board of Trade inspection. This inspection was carried out on Friday 3rd July when Major-General Hutchinson officially approved the route between Roose and Claye's Mansion in Abbey Road. Claye's Mansion later became Infield Convalescent

Home before closure and demolition in the 1960s. Infield Gardens and Infield Crescent are on the site of this mansion. This inspection allowed the tramways to be formally opened, including the section from Ramdsen Square to the Ironworks/Steelworks which did not last long due to low density of traffic. The track and sets were, however, not removed until late 1903. At the subsequent luncheon, Sir James Ramsden stated that the Corporation had been given the powers to construct the tramway but had decided to leave it to private enterprise.

It was on 11th July 1885 that the system was opened to the public with Mr William Parsons driving the first tram, the hours of work being from 8am to 10pm without a break. Rolling stock comprised eight locomotives by Kitson of Leeds and eight trailers by Falcon Works, Loughborough. These were conventional double-deck type with open sided upper decks and short canopies. Later, the top decks were enclosed by means of rather crude side covers. The seating was longitudinal and the livery was either red or maroon with white rocker panels. They were later painted one colour and covered with advertisements.

The depot was in Salthouse Road, immediately west of Vulcan Foundry, the site later being occupied by the depot of British Electric Traction Company. A tank was let into the road near the Abbey terminus for the purpose of refilling the water tanks of engines.

On 28th July 1886 on completion of the widening of the original high level bridge, the tramway to Ramsden Dock was opened. In 1897 the total route length was 5½ miles with a track length of 6 miles but all was not well financially. There were several accidents involving steam trams in the early years of operation and in August 1892 the Board of Trade wrote to the Tramway Company urging that drivers be instructed to take greater care.

In February 1893 an inspection was carried out by Major-General Hutchinson on behalf of the Board of Trade and arising from this permission was granted for further operation of the system until 11th February 1900. In October 1893 the Company asked the Corporation to obtain Parliamentary Powers to extend the tramway to Walney Ferry and an extension of the Abbey route from Claye's Mansion to the water trough at Furness Abbey. A further extension to Dalton-in-Furness was envisaged but

nothing came of these proposals. The condition of the rolling stock and the track was causing concern in 1895 and 1896 and was the subject of extensive correspondence between the Corporation and the Tramway Company culminating in January 1897 with the threat of legal action by the Corporation against the Tramway Company. In addition to the state of the rolling stock and track, there was concern over the inconvenience to passengers due to irregular running and the lack of effective management. The Company did carry out some work to address these charges.

The term 'Rapid Transit' is often associated with the 21st century but a system for Barrow was proposed as early as March 1898 when a letter was received from a Mr R Bickerdyke, Banque d'Hochelaga, Montreal, applying to the Corporation for a franchise to construct a system of lines to provide a rapid transit system throughout the Borough on the American Electric Trolley System. Mr Bickerdyke was informed that as the tramlines were in the ownership of the Tramway Company, the Corporation could not entertain his offer.

In 1898 the Company went into liquidation and although the Corporation considered purchasing it, the asking price being £22,750, in the end declined. The Company was purchased on 23rd December 1899 by British Electric Traction Limited with the intention of converting the entire system to electric traction. In the meantime, however, BET brought in two locomotives and trailers from its North Staffordshire Tramways to help maintain the services. Parliamentary powers had to be obtained for the conversion of the system, which created delay, but the Company promised to improve the steam system in the interim period.

There was a fire at the Salthouse Road Depot on the night of 27th June 1902 when several locomotives and trailers were destroyed and never replaced. Service was halted but was resumed a little later but the whole system was in such poor condition that the Board of Trade would only grant a certificate for operation, one month at a time. Locomotives and trailers were in poor condition and the badly worn track led to frequent derailments. On many occasions locomotives had to make several attempts to climb the not very steep hills at East Mount and St Georges Square, leaving a trail of sundry nuts and bolts. As well as the trams being in poor condition there were complaints regarding the dirty appearance of some conductors. Keeping clean in the continual midst of belching smoke and fumes must have been a problem.

In July 1902 the Chairman of the Tramways Committee and the Engineer were authorised to visit the Tramways Exhibition in London and to inspect the system of traction in use at Lancaster. Further visits were made by the Consultative Sub-Committee to Rothesay and Greenock to inspect cars and later to Newcastle, Gateshead, Sunderland and the Brush works at Loughborough.

The steam trams ceased operation in mid 1903 and the town had no tramway system until the commencement of electrical operation.

Clearly indicating the dilapidated state of the steam locomotives and trailers before withdrawal is this view with crew, passengers and interested onlookers. *(REC)*

Electric Trams

The Barrow in Furness Tramway Order 1903 authorised electrification of the steam system and the provision of a new tramway along Ferry Road. An entirely new permanent way was installed and the system was scheduled to be officially opened on Saturday 6th February 1904. However, on Wednesday 3rd February 1904 satisfactory speed tests were carried out with the time from the Town Hall to White House being 7½ minutes and 15 minutes from Roose to Furness Abbey. Passengers travelled free as the Company was unable to charge fares until the official permit had been received. The Barrow Herald reporting on the event stated *'it was indeed a novelty to see such beautiful cars flash noiselessly by every few minutes – all delighted with the speed with which they glided along – a foretaste of what pleasure the public would in general experience later.'*

The Abbey to Town Hall and Roose to Town Hall routes were inspected by Major Druit of the Board of Trade. He travelled from Salthouse Depot to Roose and then to the Abbey, accompanied by the Tramway Manager, Mr F Blaydon, and Councillor Dawson, Chairman of the Highways Committee, Councillor Young, the Borough Treasurer, Mr J Gunson, the Borough Engineer, Mr J W Smith and Mr Chadwick of the Town Clerk's office. Major Druit confirmed his entire satisfaction with the system and agreed to operations commencing the following morning Saturday 6th February 1904 at 8am. The initial routes were :-

Town Hall to Abbey with short workings
to White House and Hawcoat Lane
Town Hall to Roose with short workings
to Washington Hotel.

Photographed on 6th January 1909 on Roose Bridge is one of the cars numbered 8 to 12 delivered in 1904 for the Roose service which required single-deck cars to operate under Salthouse Road Bridge. A framed copy of this photograph was found in the Cumberland Motor Services Head Office in Whitehaven when it was being cleared and was kindly handed over to the author by Stagecoach at that time. *(GHC)*

Right: Three lady members of staff from tramway days display their uniforms. *(GHC)*

Unusually, for a BET tramway, the system was operated through a local Committee of Management, rather than the normal subsidiary company arrangement.

The local press was praiseworthy of the new system. The leader in the *North Western Daily Mail* proclaimied that at last Barrow had brought itself up to date with regard to public transport whilst the *Vickerstown Chronicle* declared that the streets of Barrow presented a more commercially beautiful picture than they had in the past.

There were no problems on the opening day apart from a dewirement in Ramsden Square and 9,600 passengers were carried, which was well above the number anticipated by the management. Operations were personally supervised by Mr Blaydon, the Tramways Manager. Seven cars were in use comprising four double-deck Nos. 1-4 and three single-deck Nos. 8-10. The system was of 4ft gauge generally single track with passing loops with one half mile of double track on the Ramsden Dock route. The system was complicated by having to cross the Michaelson Road bridge which had to open to allow the passage of shipping.

On 29th June 1904 electric cars were operating :-
Town Hall to Ramsden Dock with short workings to Tea House.
By about 29th October 1904 another route was operating, this being:-
Town Hall to Ferry Road.

Livery was maroon and cream but this was later changed to red and cream. The fleet at this time comprised twelve Brush tramcars, seven double-deck and five single-deck, numbered 1-7 and 8-12. These were followed the following year

Tram No. 15 dating from 1905 is shown at Ramsden Dock Station with crew. Who was the young lady with the child, possibly the wife of one of the crew? This wa**s** one of the two cars fitted with Conaty trucks which, according to the text, did not improve the riding qualities. *(STA)*

by two Raworth demi-cars numbered 13 and 14, built by Brush. Also arriving in 1905 were two double-decks, Nos. 15 and 16, which became known as the 'Rocking Horses'. Their arrival was reported thus:- *'Barrow is swaggering again because it has got two new electric cars'.* The single-decks were used on the Roose route where the low railway bridge on Salthouse Road prevented double-deck operation. The bodies and trucks on all cars were by Brush Electrical Engineering Co Ltd. The double-deck cars had a length of 15ft 4½ins with a seating capacity of 22 inside and 26 upstairs. The single-deck cars seated 24 in the centre compartment and had an open compartment at both ends, each seating seven.

These purchases reflected both increased demand coupled with poor loadings at certain times on the Roose to Ramsden Dock service.

Work commenced towards the end of 1905 on the construction of a new bridge between Barrow Island and Walney Island and replaced the ferry operated by the Furness Railway Company who had opposed the construction of the bridge because of their vested interest in the steam ferry which connected Walney Island with the mainland. The bridge was opened on 30th July 1908 and agreement had been reached for tracks to be provided over the new bridge. On 8th June 1909 a tramway service commenced to Walney Promenade, this being an extension of the previous service to Ferry Road.

This service was extended on 4th August 1911 to Biggar Bank, with short workings to Walney Promenade and Amphitrite Street. The fleet was enlarged in 1910 with the arrival of four Brush double-deck 96-seat cars numbered 17-20 for conveying shipyard workers and heavy excursion traffic for the steamers to Blackpool, Fleetwood and the Isle of Man. These cars were followed in 1911 by four single-deck Brush cars numbered 21-24, bringing the fleet total to 24. Toll monies were levied on passengers crossing Walney Bridge and these were collected by the Tramway Company with the issue of a special ½d ticket. The collection of tolls continued until 1935 when the bridge was renamed Jubilee Bridge. The fact that the structure was an opening bridge necessitated a complex arrangement for the overhead and this proved troublesome over the years.

Outbreak of the First World War in 1914 placed restriction on further expansion and also saw the introduction of women as conductresses. In 1915, two second-hand Brush cars were purchased from sister BET subsidiary, the Potteries Electric Traction Company Limited and two trailer cars were purchased in 1917 for cars 22 and 23.

During 1917 Mr W F Blaydon, who had been manager of the tramway for over 20 years, left Barrow and was replaced by Mr J Dobson, who had been assistant manager.

Tram No. 20 approaches Barrow Island from Walney Bridge. *(GHC/KNC)*

A fine crowd of officials and onlookers at Biggar Bank marking the extension of the system to Walney Island which took place on 4th August 1911. These four cars, 17-20, could carry 96 seated passengers in addition to what photographs suggest was a further considerable standing load. They were ideal for moving crowds from the shipyards or to the ferries. Advertisements on the panels demonstrate the art of the signwriter. *(REC)*

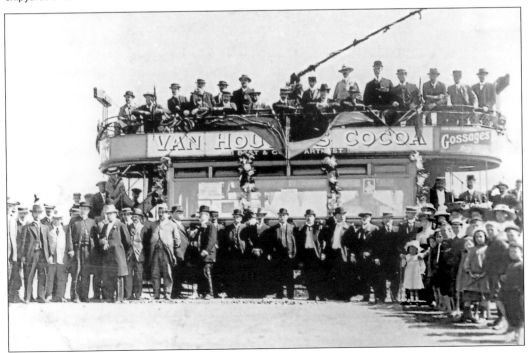

Demi-car No. 13 is shown with crew at Ramsden Dock Station. These small cars, incorporating Raworths patents, were designed to be capable of one-man-operation. Raworth was a BET Director. *(GHC)*

A photograph of staff thought to have been taken in 1915. Note the well-behaved member in the centre of the front row! *(REC)*

Corporation Tramways

On 23rd September 1919 the Corporation resolved to take up its 21 year option to purchase the tramway system from British Electric Traction Limited and this took place with effect from 1st January 1920, the cost being £96,250. Loan sanction in the sum of £107,750 was granted by the Ministry of Transport to cover the cost of setting up the undertaking. The Council passed a resolution stating that there would be no free passes issued, not even to Corporation officials, reflecting the parlous state of the finances. The fleet at takeover comprised 25 cars, a water car and a horse-drawn tower wagon. Of the cars taken over, six were considered to be beyond repair, these being Nos. 1-4, and the demi-cars 13 and 14. Number 24, one of the two 1914-built single-deckers was despatched to Coplawhill Works, with two sets of maximum traction bogies, and rebuilt

by Glasgow Corporation staff. In February 1920 it was agreed to purchase twelve new single-deck cars from Brush at a cost of £26,724. As an interim measure it was also agreed to purchase a number of second-hand cars, four of these being purchased from Southport Corporation at a cost of £325 each. It had been estimated that the cost of putting them into service would be £600 but, in fact, the eventual cost per car was £1,130. Three of the cars entered service in September and the fourth in October, in the Southport livery of crimson and cream. Six more cars came from Sheffield Corporation, these having been selected by the Barrow General Manager from a number offered for sale. The cost was £350 per car and they arrived in September, entering service in early October in the Sheffield blue and cream livery, complete with Sheffield Corporation Tramways fleet names. Acquisitions from other BET fleets were no longer on the agenda.

Photographed in Schneider Square is Tram No. 20, one of four 96 seat cars purchased in 1911 to handle the high traffic levels to and from the Shipyard, but converted, with car 19, to single-deck form in 1928. See page 10, upper photograph. *(GHC/HAW)*

In the first year of Corporation operation, 7,480,219 passengers were carried involving 606,931 car miles being operated and a loss of £671 was recorded. It was agreed in March 1921 that a standard colour scheme be adopted, this to be olive green and cream. The new cars which arrived in December 1921 were delivered in this livery. By the end of March 1922 rolling stock comprised 32 single-deck cars, nine double-deck cars, a motor-driven tower wagon, a horse-drawn tower wagon and a Ford lorry. Early in 1924 Barrow was declared to have the lowest operating cost of any municipal tramway undertaking, this being 9.96d per car mile. In 1925 vestibules were added to cars 20-2, 24 at a cost of £65 per car. This policy continued in 1926 when further cars were treated, including four of the ex-Sheffield cars.

In November 1926 an experimental bus service was commenced between the Town Hall and Tea House, operating on Saturdays and Sundays. This produced better financial results than the tram service and arising from this it was decided that trams should operate to the docks only during work times and that for the remainder of the day buses should operate from Tea House.

Screen wipers were added to trams and buses at a cost of £19 16s each in 1928 and car No. 19 was converted from double-deck to single-deck.

In 1930 consideration was given to the replacement of the tramway and an inspection was made of the trolley-bus system at Wolverhampton. However, it was eventually decided that the replacement should be by motor bus and the last tram service operated from the Abbey terminus on Tuesday 5th April 1932, three trams being used, one of which was driven by Mr William Parsons who had driven the first tram in 1885. The journey from the Town Hall to the terminus was operated by buses with the trams undertaking the return journey. Mr Thomas Smalley was the General Manager at the time. The ceremony was attended by members of the Corporation together with guests and comprised a run on the new buses to the Abbey terminus and subsequently to Biggar Bank, concluding with afternoon tea in the Town Hall.

Some of the replacement buses arrived the week before the changeover and others arrived the day before. There were teething troubles when the bus operation commenced and, despite the decrepit state of the trams, there was clamour from some sections of the public for their return. This was ruled out absolutely.

Much of the information in this chapter has been taken, with gratitude, from the books by Ian L Cormack, MA, **'Seventy Five Years on Wheels'** and **'Ninety Years on Wheels'** published by Scottish Tramway Historical Studies, and Ian Stewart's Glasgow Trams part 2 published by the STTS. Readers requiring further detailed information on the tramways of Barrow in Furness are referred to these publications.

THE MOTOR BUS

In 1914 British Electric Traction Limited, operators of the town's tramways, applied for a licence to operate a motor bus service from Barrow Town Hall to Ulverston via Dalton and this commenced in 1915. The initial vehicles were six Daimler CD models and they were followed in 1916 by three Belsize vehicles. An offer was made by BET to sell the business to the Corporation in 1919 but the offer was declined and the business passed to British Automobile Traction Limited with effect from 1st January 1920. The purchase price was £9,681 4s 9d plus stores at valuation. Three Daimler Y type were purchased in 1920 and had registrations transferred from the Belsize vehicles. Two further Daimler Y type arrived in 1920 and a further two in 1921. The service faced competition from 'jitney' operators, these being one-man operators with small lightweight vehicles who had been granted licences by Barrow Corporation and this led to a loss in revenue by BAT Ltd. In January 1922 the bus drivers of BAT Ltd came out on strike and this continued despite repeated attempts to negotiate a settlement. It was considered inadvisable to attempt to continue the service with drivers from outside the area and in March 1922 the decision was taken to close the operation in Barrow. The vehicles were removed from their garage, secretly, early one morning, and the premises vacated. The drivers arrived for picket duty only to find the depot empty and that they no longer had employment.

It is stated that the vehicles and stores that could be disposed of locally were dispersed to BAT companies at Whitehaven (Cumberland MS), Preston (Ribble MS) and Macclesfield which later became North Western Road Car Company. There are no records of such vehicles entering service with Cumberland but there are records of vehicles entering service with the other two operators.

The commencement of municipal bus operation in Barrow goes back to 1920 when first proposals for a bus service were made but it was not until 17th August 1923 that the first service was operated from Roose tram terminus to Rampside. A small Ford bus was used for this. Two small Chevrolet buses followed.

The Barrow in Furness Corporation Act 1925 contained general powers to operate bus services and an expansion of services followed. The first was an extension, in May 1925, of the Roose to Rampside service to Whitehall on the Coast Road, this being further extended along the Coast Road to Ulverston in July 1925. New Guy single-deck buses were used for this and in August 1925 two further services commenced :-

Town Hall to Ormsgill
Town Hall to Hawcoat.

Barrow Corporation operated a number of Guy B type single-deckers and this one, EO 3463 carried fleet number 1. It was on loan from Guy Motors pending delivery of Nos. 2-5 which arrived later in 1925. *(RMC)*

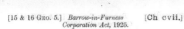

[15 & 16 Geo. 5.] *Barrow-in-Furness* [Ch cvii.]
Corporation Act, 1925.

CHAPTER cvii.

An Act to empower the mayor aldermen and A.D. 1925
burgesses of the borough of Barrow-in-Furness
to provide and work omnibuses and trolley
vehicles to make further provision with regard
to the tramways gas electricity markets and
other undertakings of the Corporation to make
provision for altering the number of councillors
and aldermen to consolidate the rates of the
borough and to make further provision with
regard to the health local government and
improvement thereof and for other purposes.
[7th August 1925.]

WHEREAS the county borough of Barrow-in-
Furness in the county palatine of Lancaster is a
municipal borough under the government of the mayor
aldermen and burgesses of the borough of Barrow-in-
Furness (in this Act called " the Corporation ") who acting
by the council are also the urban sanitary authority for
the district comprising the borough :

And whereas the Corporation are the owners of and
are working a system of tramways in the borough and it
is expedient to make further provision with regard to
the tramway undertaking of the Corporation and to
confer powers upon them for the running of omnibuses
and to empower them to provide and work mechanically
propelled vehicles adapted for use upon roads without

[*Price 4s. Net.*]   A   1

Detail from the 1925 Act

Plaque recording the opening of the new depot in January 1936 by Mrs WA Pickthall.

In October 1925 a garage was purchased in Salthouse Road, adjacent the tram depot, and this was used as the bus depot. On abandonment of the tramway, the tram depot was converted to a bus depot and this continued in use until 10th January 1936 when the new bus depot in Hindpool Road, built at a cost of £20,360, was formally opened.

In the issue dated 17th April 1928, the *Commercial Motor* magazine carried an article under the heading of :- **'Bus Activities in Barrow in Furness'**. It pointed out that with one exception, bus services operated by the Corporation, operated within the borough boundary, the exception being the service to Ulverston via the Coast Road. The list of services was quoted as follows :-

Destination	Miles	Headway	Fare
Hawcoat	2.5	20 or 30 mins	3d
Ormsgill	2.0	30 or 60 mins	2d
Roose	2.0	5 or 10 mins	2d
Rampside	5.0	2 hours	6d
Ulverston	13.0	3 to 5 trips	1s 0d
		Return Fare	1s 6d

It was pointed out that, as the last named service operated outside the borough, permission had to be sought from the Ministry of Transport and the local councils concerned to operate the service, consent being obtained in 1925. It was also reported that the Corporation had sought permission to operate to Ulverston via the main road and Dalton but this had not been granted. It was further reported that the service to Ulverston via the main road was operated on a 20 minute frequency by the Furness Omnibus Company Limited. Reference was also made to the 20 minute frequency of the service along the same route operated by Lonsdale Pullman Bus Company Limited of Ulverston, giving a combined 10 minute frequency for the service. It has been claimed that the Lonsdale vehicles were considerably more comfortable than those of their rival. Furness took over the Lonsdale Company before being taken over itself by Ribble.

Reference was made to two long distance express services from Barrow to Manchester calling at Ulverston, Carnforth, Lancaster and Preston and that the journey time was five hours. Furness Omnibus operated on Tuesdays, Thursdays and Saturdays during the summer months and Lonsdale Omnibus operated on Tuesdays and Thursdays, with some operation during the winter months. The fares quoted were 7s 0d single and 10s 0d return which compared favourably with fares of 10s 10d and £1 1s 8d respectively on the railway.

To revert to the Corporation, further expansion of services took place with the opening in 1929 of routes:-

Roose to Tea House.
North Scale to Hawcoat, and later
Old Newbarns to Town Hall and North Scale.

Early buses were lightweight single-deck models but in 1929 the almost inevitable Leyland TD1 made its appearance when four with Leyland lowbridge open-staircase bodies arrived and these were followed in 1931 by four Leyland TS3 single-deckers also with Leyland bodies.

Above: This photograph of 1929 Leyland-bodied Leyland TD1, taken when the vehicle was new clearly shows the open staircase. It was a great improvement on anything seen in Barrow until that time. *(TLP)*

Below: Leyland-bodied Leyland Tiger TS3 No 9 dating from 1931 was photographed when new. *(PCC)*

In 1930, the blue and cream livery, so long associated with Barrow, was introduced.

Reference was made in the previous chapter to the cessation of the tramways on Tuesday 5th April 1932 and this of course necessitated the purchase of replacement buses. The vehicles chosen were 18 Crossley Condor double-deckers with bodies by Northern Counties Motor and Engineering Company Limited of Wigan. The vehicles were launched at the combined ceremony covering the tramway closure and were reported on in the local press. Nine of the vehicles had petrol engines, and the other nine diesel engines, which made Barrow an early pioneer of the use of diesel engines in buses and may have influenced the choice of

Photographed when new is No. 45, one of 18 Crossley Condors with Northern Counties bodies, purchased for tramway replacement in 1932. The similarity in body outline to the Leyland 'piano fronted' bodies on Leyland TD1 chassis supplied earlier, is explained by the fact that Leyland disposed of stocks of timber parts already cut and machined to Northern Counties and Massey Brothers when it changed over to the use of metal framing in its bus bodies. *(MSC)*

Crossley as chassis supplier. The *North Western Daily Mail* reported :- '*All the vehicles are fitted with four-wheel brakes which are operated by a foot pedal. There is also a parking brake which acts on the rear wheels and is worked by hand'.* The new buses operated on the undermentioned routes. The colours refer to coloured destination screens, introduced in 1934, to readily identify routes and which were a feature of Barrow buses until the 1960s, although some of the screens continued in use on double-deck vehicles until the 1970s. They featured either white lettering on a coloured background or coloured lettering on a white background. The practice was restored in February 1990 but was phased out by 1993 in favour of high visibility yellow on a black background and electronically operated destination displays.

Abbey to Biggar Bank via Town Hall	Green
Roose to Tea House via Town Hall	Blue
Hawcoat to The Shore via Town Hall	Red
Ormsgill to Harrel Lane via Town Hall	Yellow
Cemetery to North Scale	Black/White

A new route, Oxford Street to Risedale, was introduced in 1936 and was operated by single-deck vehicles.

Following the Crossleys received in 1932 for tramway replacement, orders in the years 1933 to 1935 were split between Leyland and Crossley, bodies up to 1934 being either by Leyland or Northern Counties Motor and Engineering Co. Ltd, Wigan. In 1935 there was a change of bodybuilder to English Electric Ltd and all subsequent bodies up to 1941 were supplied by them, thus still supporting local suppliers in the county. The year 1934 had seen a return to Leyland double-deckers with the arrival of two TD3c models with Northern Counties bodies. The 'c' suffix to the chassis designations indicated that they were fitted with a torque convertor transmission system which had recently been introduced by Leyland in an attempt to simplify driving, by eliminating the need for the driver to be involved in gear changing. It was, in effect, an early form of automatic transmission and buses so fitted normally carried the words **'GEARLESS BUS'** on the radiator. The system appealed to municipal operators faced with increasing amounts of town traffic and the need to train tram drivers to drive buses. With the exception of a single Crossley Condor, supplied in 1935, Barrow standardised on this system for all subsequent deliveries up to and including 1940.

Going home. Exodus from the shipyard in the early or mid-thirties, some walking, some on cycles and some in the waiting buses. *(GHC)*

The year 1938 saw the delivery of sixteen Leyland TD5c models with bodies by English Electric, the first four being to lowbridge specification. This group photographed at English Electric Works before delivery illustrates the highbridge version of the bodywork. *(REC)*

The downside of the system was that it was less efficient in terms of fuel consumption and power output. Another factor concerned maintenance in that there were, within the unit, brass seals which needed to be perfectly smooth by patient polishing with Brasso or jewellers' rouge. Not everyone had this patience. Most operators replaced this form of transmission at the earliest opportunity which was generally during the immediate postwar years. Barrow, however, went one better than this and replaced the vehicles, all these delivered in the period 1934 to 1940 being replaced by 1950.

Following the initial deliveries with this form of transmission, subsequent deliveries comprised a single TD4c model in 1935 and four TD4c models in 1936. The 1937 delivery comprised six TD4c models and two examples of the later TD5c model. A further ten TD5c models arrived in 1938 followed by twelve in 1939 and finally six in 1940. Clearly by now Barrow had a very modern bus fleet.

Wartime

The Second World War was declared on 3rd September 1939 and the effect on fuel supplies was immediate, resulting in restrictions in the operation of services. The effect on vehicle deliveries was not so immediate and orders which had been placed before the outbreak of hostilities were generally fulfilled as indicated above with the 1940 deliveries and a further four Leyland TD7 in 1941. These four examples had bodies to English Electric design but were built by East Lancashire Coachbuilders of Blackburn.

The winter of 1940 was notorious for the amount of snow which fell and Barrow certainly received its share. It is reported that two double-deckers were stranded on the coast road, because of the snow, for a period of three weeks. Crews worked very hard with shovels to free the vehicles.

To return to the question of vehicle supplies, restrictions were applied and regular manufacturers including Leyland Motors (and English Electric) were prevented from bus manufacture with their output being directed at the war effort. Initially, stocks of components were 'frozen' but it was then realised that buses were needed to get workers to the factories and other places of employment and these stocks were 'unfrozen'. A limited number of chassis were manufactured from these components

A view showing two double-deckers with other vehicles stranded on the Coast Road in the winter of 1940/41. *(PCC)*

and in 1942 Barrow received three Leyland TD7 models, one with East Lancashire body and the other two with bodies by Brush. All the TD7 models had the conventional clutch and gearbox.

In the further realisation of the need for buses during wartime, the Government authorised Guy Motors of Wolverhampton to design and build a double-deck chassis and placed an initial order for 500. Guy had not built double-deck chassis in quantity for some years and they designed a very simple but rugged chassis to be powered by either a 5-cylinder or 6-cylinder Gardner engine and designated as Guy Arab I. A standard utility body was designed to the requirements of the Ministry of Supply, devoid of all frills, including provision of slatted wooden seats. The supply of buses was strictly controlled by the Ministry of War Transport and operators had to accept what was available in terms of quantity and manufacturers. A number of firms were authorised to build the bodies to this standard specification.

Barrow was allocated six Guy Arab I chassis in 1942 and these had bodies by Park Royal of London. These vehicles and all subsequent wartime vehicles allocated to Barrow, with one exception, had 5-cylinder Gardner engines. This was no doubt influenced by the generally flat

terrain around Barrow whereas further north in Whitehaven, Cumberland Motor Services, in an area of hilly terrain, was allowed to purchase 6-cylinder examples. Later, Daimler was authorised to build bus chassis and Barrow received two CWG5 examples in 1943 along with a further three Guy Arab 1 models. In 1944 another Guy

Massey-bodied Daimler CWG5 No. 92 was new in 1943 but was withdrawn and sold to W North, dealer as early as July 1950 and was photographed at the dealer's yard in August 1950. It was sold for further service to W & H Everett – Ideal Services, South Kirkby – in December 1950 and served that company until March 1953. *(PTC)*

arrived but this was to the later Arab II specification and was provided with a 6-cylinder engine. It was the only utility double-deck body supplied to Barrow with wooden seats. All the vehicles supplied in 1943 and 1944 had bodies by Massey Bros, Wigan to the standard wartime specification. Drivers must have found it quite a challenge handling the Guys with their notorious crash gearboxes after the Leylands, the great majority of which were of the 'gearless' type. Furthermore, the gearboxes of the Arab models had a gate which was the opposite way round to convention in that first and second gears were to the right of the gate and third and fourth to the left. The author recalls the Cumberland Guy Arab I vehicles being provided with a notice in the cab to warn drivers of this arrangement. Perhaps the most apt description of the transmission is given by Robin Hannay and Stuart Broatch in the book **'80 Years of Guy Motors Limited'**, published by Venture Publications. We quote from it :-

'The transmission of the wartime Arab was a fine piece of vintage machinery, the origins of which went back to the late 1920s. Even the double plate clutch was rather dated by the early 1940s and the unusual about-face gear shift pattern was retained. What mattered was that, despite its somewhat vintage specification in some areas, the wartime Arab showed itself to be an excellent design.'

The fact that Barrow received so many 'unfrozen' and wartime vehicles is a clear reflection of the importance of Vickers in the war effort.

The other wartime intake at Barrow comprised new bodies for three Leyland TS3 single-deckers dating from 1931 and four Leyland TS4 single-deckers dating from 1933. The new bodies were supplied by East Lancashire Coachbuilders which in itself was something of a surprise as normally all wartime rebodies for single-deckers were supplied by H V Burlingham of Blackpool. There was some similarity of outline to the Burlingham bodies indicating compliance with a wartime standard design. A notable difference was the use of window pans, brought about by the fact that East Lancashire Coachbuilders continued to use metal framing for

Leyland TS4 No. 3 dating from 1933 was re-bodied by East Lancashire Coachbuilders in 1943 and remained in service until September 1954. *(RM)*

their bodies during wartime. At this time the main function of East Lancashire Coachbuilders was the rebodying of double-deckers and for some reason, which has never been clarified, they continued to build to their prewar design rather than to the standard wartime specification.

Whilst the chassis were rugged and served the industry well, the same could not be said of the bodies which tended to deteriorate quickly. This was no reflection on the body builders but was due to the poor quality unseasoned timber which was available. The exception to this was bodies built by East Lancashire Coachbuilders, for reasons mentioned above, and also those built by Northern Counties who were allowed to continue with partial metal framing, albeit to the outline of the standard wartime specification. Arising from this, many operators found it necessary to carry out major rebuilding of these bodies, or in some cases rebodying, in the immediate postwar period. A notable exception to this was Stockport Corporation where the entire wartime allocation comprised 16 Massey-bodied Guy Arab IIs rather than a mix of chassis and body makes received by most operators at this time. Furthermore, Stockport had 18-20 years of service out of these vehicles with little evidence of major rebuilding having taken place. This did not happen at Barrow as we shall see in the next section.

Postwar

In the postwar period it took most operators many years to recover from the restrictions of wartime with the result that they were operating prewar and wartime vehicles into the late 'fifties and early 'sixties. This was not the situation at Barrow where the Corporation took delivery of 70 new double-deckers between 1948 and 1951 thus providing complete replacement of the double-deck fleet and providing Barrow with what must have been one of the most modern, if not the most modern, municipal bus fleet in the country. Renewal started in 1948 with the arrival of 20 Crossley DD42 double-deckers with Crossley bodies and this in itself was a significant order for an operator the size of Barrow. Ten of the Crossleys, although finished in Barrow livery and with Barrow style of destination displays, had interior details similar to vehicles being supplied by Crossley to Manchester Corporation Transport. These included red seating with match strikers marked MCTD on the back of the upper saloon seats. It is possible that these were diverted from a Manchester order but as Manchester was busy with fleet renewal at this time, this seems unlikely. The other possibility is that Crossley offered an

The first postwar double-deckers to be received were ten Crossley-bodied Crossleys which arrived in 1948 numbered 40-49. The last of these is shown at Michaelson Road. *(RM)*

earlier delivery and possibly a price reduction if Barrow accepted interior details to the Manchester specification. There was reference in the local press to the Crossleys and the writer referred to the red seats and wide gangways. When Manchester had placed the order for their Crossleys, the maximum width was 7ft 6ins but when this was increased to 8ft 0ins Manchester decided to change to the new permissible width. In order to minimise the increase in cost and to provide greater gangway width, it was decided to utilise the seats intended for 7ft 6ins wide vehicles but to provide longer cushions for these. This explains why the cushions extended beyond the seat frames.

However, there was more to come and 1949 saw the arrival of 30 Leyland PD2 models with bodies by Park Royal, also built to the recently authorised greater width of 8ft 0ins. This combination of chassis and body was to become the Barrow standard for years to come with ten examples arriving in 1950 and a further ten in 1951. This provided Barrow with not only a modern fleet, but a largely standardised fleet which must have been the envy of many a fleet engineer. There was an interesting connection between Barrow and Park Royal dating back to

The second batch of ten Crossley double-deckers received in 1948 were numbered 101-10 and No. 107 is shown here. *(TLP)*

circa 1908, when one Bill Black, by now Sir William and PRV's boss, had worked for Vickers, Barrow, in the early days of his career. Withdrawal of prewar vehicles commenced in 1948 with the arrival of the Crossleys and the withdrawal of the

Park Royal-bodied Leyland PD2 No. 124, from 1949, clearly shows the Barrow custom of using large white fleet numbers, on or adjacent to the driver's door. (HPC)

wartime vehicles commenced as early as 1949 when they were only seven years old, when the first Certificate of Fitness expired.

On 11th April 1950 alterations were made to the Ormsgill – Harrel Lane and Oxford Street – Risedale Road services, introducing a Circular service Oxford Street – Harrel Lane and Town Hall circle via Friars Lane and Oxford Street while Ormsgill was linked to the Risedale Road route. It was about this time that double-deck buses were introduced to the former Oxford Street – Risedale Road, now Ormsgill – Risedale Road route, as this had been previously worked by single-deck buses, because of the steep Greengate Hill. This may reflect the fact that the 'Gearless' buses had a reputation of not being very good on hills. Needless to say, the double-deck Leyland PD2 models, with their powerful engines, had no problem with the hill. Also at this time, the Roose route was modified to one bus in three going to Roose (Ship Inn). On 1st February 1953, this service was extended to a new housing estate at Newbarns.

The business of the Grange Motor and Cycle Company Limited was acquired, jointly with Ribble Motor Services, in 1951. This company had operated on the Barrow to Ulverston service in accordance with an agreement drawn up between Barrow Corporation, Grange Motor and Cycle Company and Ribble Motor Services, dated 19th

Massey-bodied Leyland Royal Tiger No. 52 new in 1955 and photographed for the bodybuilders at that time. Note the high back coach seating. *(STA)*

September 1938. This Agreement was modified with effect from 18th October 1951 to take account of the demise of Grange Motor Company. Barrow did not participate in the operation of the additional workings involved.

The early 'fifties saw great changes in single-deck design with the introduction of underfloor-engined chassis. This arrangement allowed the full length of the bus to be used to accommodate passengers and coupled to the recently introduced maximum length to 30ft enabled a seating capacity of 44 or 45. Furthermore, the fact that the entrance could be provided immediately opposite the driver's cab made the layout readily adaptable for single person operation, a feature that was to figure prominently in the coming years. Barrow's first examples of such vehicles were two Leyland Royal Tigers with Leyland bodies which arrived in 1952. A further example, but with body by Massey Bros of Wigan, arrived in 1955. The first conversion to one-man operation took place on 6th October 1958 on the service from Barrow to Ulverston via the Coast Road.

The following year, 1956, saw the withdrawal of the first of the Crossleys, nine examples being withdrawn, when they were only eight years old.

Further withdrawal of Crossleys saw one depart in 1957 and five more in 1958, leaving only five of the original 20 still in service and these were withdrawn in 1959. Further new double-deckers arrived in 1958, and again Park Royal-bodied Leyland PD2 models were favoured with ten examples being purchased. This meant that following the withdrawal of the final five Crossleys in 1959, all double-deck vehicles in the fleet were Park Royal-bodied Leyland PD2 models. The final ten carried the later Park Royal body design, with framework in aluminium alloy, and were to be the last such examples to be purchased as we shall see later. A further underfloor-engined single-deck arrived in 1959 but was to the lighter Leyland Tiger Cub design, again with body by Massey Bros.

A further investment in the fleet took place in 1959 when the ten Leyland PD2s supplied in 1950 and numbered 141–150 were rebodied by Chas H Roe of Leeds, then owned by Park Royal. This action seems to have arisen from the fact that there was deterioration of the timber framework of the

Leyland TS4 No. 2 delivered in 1933 was re-bodied by East Lancashire Coachbuilders in 1943 and then converted to a mobile clinic for the Health Department in 1952. It was finally withdrawn in November 1964 when the chassis was over 30 years old and the wartime body over 20 years old. Quite a creditable life span. *(TLP)*

Heading along Michaelson Road is 1958 Leyland PD2 No. 167 with the later style of Park Royal body. *(TLP)*

The ten Park Royal-bodied Leyland PD2s delivered in 1950 and numbered 141-150 were re-bodied by Chas H Roe in 1959 or 1960 and No. 144 is shown here after rebodying. Behind is a Leyland PD2 with its original Park Royal body from the batch delivered in 1951. *(TLP)*.

original bodies. The same problem was not likely to occur in the new bodies as builder Chas H Roe were, at that time, still using teak for the lower saloon and aluminium alloy for the upper saloon framework and had a reputation for solidarity. Two of these, numbers 147 and 148 were fitted with electrically-operated platform doors and were used on the Barrow to Ulverston service operated jointly with Ribble Motor Services.

In its issue dated 23rd September 1960 the *Commercial Motor* magazine reported that two Corporations, Barrow and Salford, were in danger of being expelled from the Federation of Municipal Transport Employers, having been charged with offering additional incentives to their staff outside the terms of the nationally agreed wages structure. It was alleged that heated views were held on the question of extra incentives but the principle of the same rate for the same job had become increasingly difficult to apply. It was pointed out that in Barrow in Furness municipal transport pay was regulated, indirectly but inevitably, by Vickers.

A return to double-deck purchases was made in 1961 with the arrival of a further ten Leyland PD2 models. However, by this time Park Royal had discontinued production of their elegant body design which had been fitted to the 1959 order and substituted what has often been described

Massey-bodied Leyland PD2 No. 4, one of the batch of 10 purchased in 1961 and numbered 1-10, thus starting a new series of fleet numbering for double-deckers. They were renumbered 101-110 in 1970. This photograph, taken for Massey Brothers at the time of delivery, illustrates the elegant lines of the body. *(STA)*

Photographed at the handover of the Massey-bodied Leyland PD2s are Mr Albert Burrows, the Barrow General Manager, at the extreme right and to his right Mr Arthur Tyldesley, Managing Director of Massey Brothers, together with other representatives of the Council. *(STA)*

as the ugliest double-deck body of the period. Arising from this a number of regular Park Royal customers looked elsewhere for body supplies, many turning to either Massey Bros or East Lancashire Coachbuilders. Barrow chose the former and not only was there a change in builder but also a change in layout in that forward entrances were specified. Massey Bros lived up to their well established reputation and produced ten well proportioned and well finished attractive bodies. The Massey metal-framed body had an excellent reputation for quality and these vehicles proved to be a good buy for Barrow giving around 20 years service. They were initially numbered 1-10 but were renumbered 101-110 in 1970. These were to be the last double-deck buses to be purchased by Barrow for over 20 years. From 1963 to 1980 all vehicles purchased were to be single-deck and no longer would vehicles be purchased in the large quantities of the immediate postwar years.

Initially, Barrow remained faithful to Leyland Motors for chassis, purchasing Leyland Leopard L1 type with East Lancashire Coachbuilders dual-doorway bodies, six examples being supplied in 1963. Thereafter, the chassis type was the PSU3 or PSU3A with five examples in 1966, Nos. 50-4, five in 1967, 55-9, five in 1968, 60-4 and five in 1969, 45-9. The bodies for the 1966 examples were supplied by Strachans, a new make for Barrow, but all the others were bodied

Heading for the Ship Inn on 6th July 1972, Leyland Leopard L1 No. 71. The severe frontal aspect, caused partly by the angling of the windscreen to reduce reflections, does little to improve the overall appearance of the bodywork. *(RD)*

On Michaelson Road leading towards the High Level bridge on 27th September 1979 *en route* to Tea House is East Lancashire-bodied Leyland Leopard No. 60. The wrap-around front screen improves both the appearance and the drivers visibility. *(RD)*

The Leyland Leopards were serving the town well but, in an attempt to provide easier access for passengers, five Daimler Fleetlines with East Lancashire bodies were purchased in 1971 and numbered 1-5. Shown at Ulverston, awaiting departure to Barrow on 6th July 1972, is No. 1. The low driving position sits uneasily on the rest of the body. *(RD)*

This Plaxton-bodied Bedford VAM70 coach, acquired from North Star Coaches Ltd, of Stevenage in 1971 and numbered 80, is shown at Blackpool on 1st August 1975. *(MB)*

by East Lancashire Coachbuilders, although the five supplied in 1967, were built by Neepsend Coachworks, Sheffield, an associate company of East Lancashire Coachbuilders who built these bodies to East Lancs designs. The Leyland Leopard was a well respected, reliable solid chassis but the problem with it being underfloor-engined, was that it resulted in a high floor layout at a time when low floor layouts were becoming popular. It was not surprising, therefore, that in 1971, an order was placed for five Daimler Fleetline single-deck chassis with bodies by East Lancashire Coachbuilders. Leyland had introduced their Panther rear-engined single-deck model, which accommodated a low floor body, but it was not one of Leyland's finest models and was certainly not held in the same high esteem as the Leopard. Also in 1971, an unusual vehicle entered the fleet in the form of a Bedford VAM70 chassis with coach body by Plaxton. Although owned by the Transport Department, it was used mainly by the Social Services Department.

E N Hadwin, Ulverston

The local coach business of EN Hadwin of Ulverston, established since about 1916, was purchased with effect from 7th January 1973 and involved ten coaches, all with Bedford chassis and Duple bodies, numbered H1–H10, details of which are given in the Fleet Summary. The acquisition was announced in the *Evening* Mail dated Friday 17th January 1973 under the heading **'COUNCIL NOW IN LUXURY TRAVEL BUSINESS'.** A joint statement issued by Mr EN Hadwin and Barrow Corporation Transport Department said that the coaches would continue to operate under the name Hadwin's Luxury Coaches, would retain Hadwin's livery and would, in the main, be operated by the same staff.

In 1975 numbers H1–H4 were withdrawn and replaced by three Bedford YRT models with Duple bodies. The operation continued to function as a separate entity under the name of Hadwin (Tours) Limited, Ulverston, but was short-lived and was subsequently sold to Shaw's of Silverdale in March 1977.

Duple-bodied Bedford YRT No. H2 was one of three purchased new in 1975 for the Hadwin fleet. It was photographed at Southport on 19th August 1976. *(RD)*

Photographed in Ramsden Square on 6th July 1972 is Park Royal-bodied Leyland PD2, one of ten received in 1958 and by now carrying the later livery. *(RD)*

The Leyland National

The National Bus Company came into being with effect from 1st January 1969 and this brought together companies which had previously been in the Tilling Group and those from the British Electric Traction Federation. Locally, this included Ribble Motor Services and further north, Cumberland Motor Services.

Arising from this, an association was set up between Leyland Bus and the National Bus Company to design and build a standard single-deck bus which was intended to suit all requirements. A purpose built factory was erected at Lillyhall, West Cumberland, to build the vehicle which was to be of standard design with very little variation in specification allowed. Subsidiary companies of the National Bus Company had no choice and had to use the model, which became known as the Leyland National, for their single-deck requirements.

The intention had been that it would also be attractive to municipal and private operators together with the export market. There was, however, very limited response from these markets. One of the problems with it was the 500 series engine which Leyland had developed for the model. It gained a reputation of being noisy, dirty and inefficient with regard to fuel consumption. Furthermore, the internal finish to the body was somewhat spartan and soon became shabby. In

an attempt to boost sales, Leyland withdrew the popular Bristol RE low-floor single-deck chassis, Bristol having become part of the Leyland empire.

Barrow became one of the few municipal operators to purchase the Leyland National with five arriving in 1974, two of which were classed as 'dual-purpose' with coach seating. These were followed by another five in 1977 and a further two in 1978. There were reliability problems with these buses, mainly related to the engine which compared very unfavourably with the Gardner engines fitted to the Daimler Fleetlines. A return to Gardner engines was made in 1979 with the purchase of two Dennis Dominators with bodies by East Lancashire Coachbuilders. The original Leyland National, retrospectively dubbed the National 1, was succeeded by the Leyland National 2, the main advantage of this later model being the abandonment of the 500 series engine which had been the subject of so much criticism. The replacement was the O680 series engine as used by Leyland in other bus chassis. Barrow purchased four Leyland National 2 models in 1980. The following year, 1981, saw the withdrawal of the last two Massey-bodied

Leyland National, No. 7 was one of the first of the breed to enter service in Barrow. It was photographed on 14th August 1986 on Abbey Road, passing the railway station heading for Biggar Bank. A distinctive feature of this new model was the large roof-mounted air conditioning pod at the rear of the new vehicle. *(HP)*

Leyland PD2 models meaning that Barrow now had an entirely single-deck fleet, but this was a situation which was soon to change.

Traditionally, Barrow buses had not displayed service numbers and the Leyland Nationals were the first vehicles to be supplied with this facility. This no doubt arose from the fact that the National had a very rigid specification with the result that operators received what the manufacturer thought they should have, rather than what the operator wanted. This is borne out by the fact that the Dennis Dominators did not have the facility for service numbers. The only other new vehicles to be supplied with service number blinds were the Leyland Atlanteans referred to later.

This inflexible approach even extended to colour schemes where, initially, only Poppy Red, Leaf Green or White (the three NBC colours) were available. The computerised paint shop was not designed to accommodate any other colours. With such 'advanced' thinking was it any wonder that the Leyland National plant could never achieve its planned output? The local newspaper, the *North West Evening Mail* reported on 7th January 1981 that the use of conductors and conductresses on the Corporation buses would cease in favour of one-person-operation in order to reduce costs. The newspaper reported on the longest serving

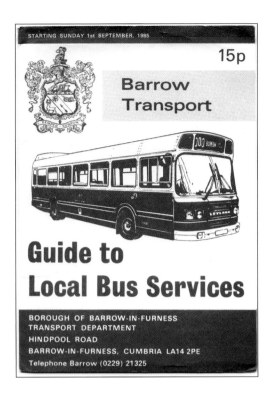

conductress, Mrs Joyce Whitehead of Ormsgill, who had worked on the buses for 21 years. Joyce had worked with her husband John on the same duties since 1965.

Leaving the Town Hall for Ulverston via the Coast Road on 14th August 1986 is Leyland National No. 17, one of two delivered in 1978. Who applied the livery is uncertain, but what is sure that it could not have been painted at the Lillyhall factory. *(HP)*

The Return of the Double-Decker

The period without double-deck operation was to be very brief for, in December 1982 two Leyland Fleetline double-deckers were purchased. By now, Daimler was part of the Leyland empire and what had been the Daimler Fleetline was renamed Leyland Fleetline. The vehicles had been new to London Transport in 1976 and were therefore only six years old when acquired from Ensign (dealer) in Purfleet who had converted them from dual to single door. The Daimler Fleetline was a popular chassis which had found favour throughout the country but was not popular with London Transport, hence the early withdrawal. Another purchase in 1982 from Ensign was a Leyland National 1 which had originally been No. 26 in the Plymouth fleet, before passing to EE Young of Rampton. It was acquired for spares and the engine and gearbox were transferred to No. 8 in 1982.

The first new double-deckers for 22 years arrived in 1983 and comprised three Leyland Atlantean AN68D models with bodies by Northern Counties. They were followed by a similar example in 1984. Also acquired in 1984 were a further two ex-London Transport Leyland Fleetlines which were again acquired via Ensign who converted them to single door. These were the last vehicles to be purchased by Barrow Corporation Transport Department.

Following the purchase of the three DMS Fleetlines, a further two were purchased in 1984 and numbered 108/9. The first of these was photographed in Abbey Road on 14th August 1986. *(HP)*

Barrovian Travel

A further attempt at establishing a coaching operation came in 1986 when two coaches were purchased and the name Barrovian Travel was chosen for the operation which commenced in May 1986.

The End of an Era

The Transport Act 1985 included the privatisation of the National Bus Company, the deregulation of bus services and the option for municipal operators to either sell to a private company or form 'arms length' limited liability companies. Barrow chose this second option and Barrow Borough Transport Limited was formed. In preparation for this situation there was correspondence and meetings with Ribble, particularly with regard to the Agreement for the joint operation of the Barrow to Ulverston via Dalton service. In a letter from Mr IAE Chapman, Managing Director, dated 8th July 1986, it was proposed by Ribble that, having regard to the consequences of the 1985 Transport Act, this Agreement be terminated with effect from midnight on 25th October 1986 by mutual consent. Mr DGB Lyon, Town Clerk and Chief Executive of Barrow Borough Council, confirmed agreement to this in his reply dated 10th July 1986.

Photographed at 11pm on 25th October 1986 with Inspector Dave Attwood driving is 1958 Leyland PD2 No. 169 operating the last service to Harrel Lane via Abbey Road. *(PCC)*

Parked at the Town Hall stop awaiting departure to West Shore on 10th April 1985 is Northern Counties-bodied Leyland Atlantean No. 106. Someone is trying to join John Cleese at the Ministry of Funny Walks! *(HP)*

BARROW BOROUGH TRANSPORT LIMITED

A new era began on 26th October 1986, a date often referred to as 'Deregulation Day', when Barrow Borough Transport Limited commenced operation as an 'arms length' limited company with Barrow Borough Council as the only shareholder. It inherited 41 vehicles from the previous operation which was only about half the number of vehicles in the Corporation fleet at its heyday in the late 'fifties and early 'sixties. This very much reflected the changing times throughout the country over the previous 25 years or so, a situation largely brought about by increasing car ownership.

Mr D Gwynn, who had been General Manager and Engineer of Barrow Corporation Transport retired, and just days before the new company was to commence operation a Managing Director, Mr D Bowen, was appointed. A Chief Engineer,

Mr C Connell, was appointed and some time afterwards Mr John Garrett was appointed Company Secretary. Day to day management of the Company rested with these three gentlemen, none of whom had previous experience in the passenger transport industry. Mr D Hustings had been Chief Traffic Assistant and he was appointed Traffic Manager for the new operation. Mr Hustings had joined Barrow Corporation in 1973 when the business of Hadwin's coaches, with whom he had been employed, was taken over. His knowledge of bus operations in Barrow was therefore considerable.

Operators had to register services in February 1986 which they intended to operate on a commercial basis, with effect from Deregulation Day, 26th October 1986. Where operators considered that services could not be operated on a commercial basis, ie at a profit, the local transport authority, in this case Cumbria County Council, could invite tenders from operators for the operation of such services if they were

An East Lancashire-bodied Leyland Leopard, No. 61 is parked at the Town Hall on 27th December 1986 illustrates the BBT name as applied to these vehicles. *(RD)*

Travelling along Abbey Road passing the railway rtation and heading for the town centre on 6th May 1987, Leyland National No. 17 shows the BBT name as applied to the Leyland Nationals. *(HP)*

considered to be socially desirable. Barrow Borough Transport registered services as follows:-

BARROW BOROUGH TRANSPORT LIMITED – SERVICES REGISTERED FOR DEREGULATION DAY.

Biggar Bank Walney Island, Town Centre, Greystone Estate, Dalton	M-S No evenings
Holbeck Farm, Holbeck Park Avenue, Town Centre, North Scale	M-S Evenings
Lakes Parade, Hawcoat, Town Centre, Newbarns	M-S No evenings
Ravenglass Road, Town Centre, North Scale	M-S No evenings
Lesh Lane, Newbarns, Town Centre, West Shore	M-S Evenings
Holbeck Farm, Holbeck Park Avenue, Town Centre, Tea House	M-S No evenings
Flass Lane/Harrel Lane, Town Centre, West Shore	Daily
Middlefield, Ormsgill, Town Centre, Lesh Lane, Newbarns	Daily
Biggar Bank, Town Centre, Lakes Parade, Hawcoat	Daily
Middlefield, Ormsgill, Town Centre, Flass Lane/Harrel Lane	Daily

In addition, several works and schools services were registered.

Things were now to be very different from what they had been in previous years. The 1985

Poster showing a more commercial awareness.

Illustrating the BBT name as applied to the Leyland Atlanteans and also the later livery is No. 107 awaiting departure to Tea House from the Town Hall on 27th December 1986. *(RD)*

Transport Act had brought about two major changes, the first being the sale of the National Bus Company and the second the deregulation of bus services which meant that existing operators no longer enjoyed the protection which they had experienced under the 1930 Transport Act. Under the new Act, other operators could register services in parallel with existing services. It was this second effect which was to have a major influence in Barrow.

Up to this time, Ribble Motor Services had operated inter-urban and rural services from a depot in Ulverston but were now attracted to the possibilities in the operation of Town Services in a town as large as Barrow. In February 1986 Ribble had lost profitable city services in Carlisle following the takeover by Cumberland of the Carlisle and Penrith areas from Ribble.

Prior to deregulation, Barrow had worked jointly with Ribble on the service to Ireleth, on the service to Ulverston via Dalton and on the Coast Road service to Ulverston. Ribble obtained by tender the Coast Road service and became the sole operator on the service to Ulverston via Dalton. This provided further competition for Barrow who now operated no further than Dalton. Arising from this the fleet size was further reduced from 41 to 31.

Leyland National 2 No. 20 parked at Greenodd on 10th September 1987 whilst driver Eddie Flynn had his lunch, before proceeding to Windermere to pick up passengers on the day excursion service that Barrow operated at that time. *(RD)*

In late 1986, shortly after the commencement of operations, Barrow issued an advert for a 'Christmas Cracker'. This offered, for the period 1st December to 24th December 1986, a special return fare of 40 pence available on any BBT bus after 9am. This gave rise to complaints from Ribble who took the matter up with the Office of Fair Trading, claiming that the fare was totally uneconomic and regarded as predatory.

Barrow in Lakeland

Barrow now recognised that it was up against it and attempted to retaliate against Ribble by joining forces with Lancaster City Transport, which had also experienced increased operation by Ribble into its traditional territory, and introduced services in Kendal. The services commenced on 30th November 1987 and Barrow provided a service to Kendal via Dalton, Ulverston and Grange over Sands which operated three times per day and provided positioning facilities for staff and vehicles. Barrow used Leyland Nationals on the service which was numbered 3 and destination displays were modified to suit the new services. Barrow provided much of the publicity material and the Town Services operated in Kendal, jointly with Lancaster were :-

Route 8 Kendal – Windermere Road – Hall Garth – Burneside Road – Kendal

Route 9 Kendal – Railway Station – Sandylands Estate.

Each service operated every 15 minutes, Mondays to Saturdays. Very early in the operation Barrow decided that it did not wish to continue and

gave notice to the Traffic Commissioner to cease the service on 6th February 1988. By contrast, Lancaster was much more enthusiastic even to the extent of opening a sub depot in the town and providing additional services to Ambleside. The Lancaster operations continued until 29th July 1989 on Town Services and until 2nd September 1989 on the service to Ambleside.

Arrival of the Minibuses

The other action taken by Barrow was the introduction of minibuses, the first being five Dodge S56 with coachbuilt bodies by East Lancashire Coachbuilders, two of which were dual-purpose. They were numbered 82-86 and registered D456-60 BEO. However, due to the chassis numbers on the registration documents being different to those on the vehicles, the registration plates had to be exchanged to ensure agreement of chassis numbers. This exchange was carried out in December 1987, a year after the vehicles entered service. A further Dodge S56, but with body by Reeve Burgess, also with coach seating, arrived in 1987. In 1988 14 Talbot Pullman six-wheeled minibuses arrived, these being on lease, and offering the advantage of a low floor with easier access than conventional minibuses. This easier access was welcomed by passengers and Ribble responded by bringing into Barrow ten similar vehicles which had been taken over with the United Transport Zippy operation in Preston and Bee Line Buzz operations in Manchester.

Awaiting departure from the Town Hall to Newbarns on 5th October 1988 is East Lancashire-bodied Dodge S56 minibus No. 82. *(HP)*

With examples of the competition from Ribble in the background, Talbot minibus No. 90 awaits departure from the Town Hall to Biggar Bank on 24th December 1988. *(RD)*

NORTH-WEST Evening Mail

Est. 1898 ———————— Monday, March 28, 1988 ————————

BUS BOSS QUITS IN STORM

PROFIT-HUNGRY Barrow Borough Transport has lost a senior member of its management team after a boardroom row.

The company's traffic manager, Mr David Hustings, stormed out after what company secretary John Garrett today described as a 'policy disagreement'.

Mr Hustings joined the former Barrow Corporation Transport Department in 1975 after the undertaking took over the Hadwin's coach business.

Previously he had been with Grey Green Coaches in London.

PRIVATE

His sudden departure comes as the new privatised company is struggling to reach break-even and wipe out a £300,000 loss.

Private coach hire has been one of the company's profitable enterprises from the start.

Mr Hustings was not

Traffic chief walks out after boardroom row

at his Ireleth home today. At the Hindpool Road depot all Mr Garrett would say was: 'There was a policy disagreement and Mr Hustings has left.

REPLACED

'This was last Thursday and I am not prepared to make any more comment.

'It was a general management disagreement, but I would rather not go into that.'

Asked if Mr Hustings would be replaced, he said: 'I think he probably will, in a slightly different form.'

The company is currently undergoing a major re-organisation of maintenance schedules and popular 'mini' and 'midi' bus

operations are being extended.

COACH

Practically the whole of the losses so far have been attributed to ordinary bus-stop services.

The former corporation service took over Hadwins in 1973 to launch into the private coach hire business, but four years later sold off the business, amid a storm of protest, for £55,000.

But with the experience gained the department maintained a small private hire arm which has been developed up to the present day and now forms an important part of BBT operations

On Monday 28th March 1988, the *North West Evening Mail* carried the headline **'Bus Boss Quits in Storm – Traffic chief walks out after boardroom row'**. This related to the fact that Mr David Hustings had been dismissed. Two months later on Saturday 28th May 1988 the same newspaper carried another headline :- **'All change as Ribble grab the man BBT kicked out - Sacked bus boss joins the opposition.'** It reported that Mr Hustings had been appointed Operations Officer for the Furness area.

There were further management developments reported in the Evening Mail on 3rd August 1988 stating that Mr David Bowen had resigned his position as Managing Director due to ill health. Councillor Jack Biggins, the Board Chairman,

stated that the Board had still to decide what to do about a replacement but that in the meantime the Company would be under the control of Mr John Garrett, Company Secretary, who at that time had only been with the Company eight months.

On 6th September 1988 there was a complaint from Ribble to the Office of Fair Trading stating that Barrow Borough Transport had registered additional services to commence on 4th September which the Traffic Commissioner had accepted for commencement on 9th September 1988. In the meantime, Barrow had commenced operating the services on or about 4th or 5th August. Ribble had eventually contacted the acting General Manager at Barrow who acknowledged that the operations were illegal but his solution had been to continue to operate the services without charging fares. Ribble's claim was that the action of Barrow Borough Transport was causing damage to their business.

The Beginning of the End

Despite various efforts, the writing was very much 'on the wall' for Barrow Borough Transport. A proposal for a management/employee co-operative buyout was made in October 1988 and was approved in principle by the Borough Council and the trade unions but was not proceeded with. Examination of the accounts had indicated that the Company was steadily losing money and had been since privatisation with a loss to date of almost £1 million. At a hearing in the High Court in Manchester on 21st December 1988, two partners from Price Waterhouse were appointed as joint administrators. The administration order handed control of the company to these two partners and a period of three months was granted to enable the Company to prove to creditors that it could make a profit. The order protected the Company from being placed into liquidation by its creditors within this three month period. It was stated that a meeting of creditors would be held before 21st March 1989 when the administrators would be bound to put proposals for the future of the Company before the creditors for approval.

A report in the *North West Evening Mail* on 12th January 1989 stated that Barrow Borough Transport had been offered for sale and that more than 20 prospective purchasers had expressed interest. It had been advertised in the financial press a few days earlier.

The meeting with creditors duly took place on 2nd February 1989 when a packed meeting was told that if neither of the two interested parties came forward, it would be in the creditors best interests for the Company to cease trading. At this stage, the two companies thought to be interested in purchasing Barrow Borough Transport Limited were Ribble Motor Services and Preston Bus. Ribble was not yet part of the Stagecoach and Stagecoach and Lancaster City Transport were reported to have denied any interest.

With the uncertain future of Barrow Borough Transport, Ribble began accepting BBT concessionary passes on their vehicles with effect from 7th April 1989. Ribble then introduced new passes from week commencing 10th April 1989 along with considerable publicity in an attempt to get BBT pass holders to change. The joint administrators of BBT stated that they could not issue new concessionary passes but that passes due to expire on 31st March 1989 would remain valid until further notice.

Away from Barrow an interesting development took place with effect from Friday 21st April 1989 when Ribble Motor Services Limited was taken over by Stagecoach. This was to have significant effect on Barrow as we see later.

It was reported that on 4th May 1989 a prospective purchaser was ready to exchange contracts for the purchase of Barrow Borough Transport but the MP for Barrow, Mr Cecil Franks, demanded an investigation into what was claimed to be an irregularity concerning Barrow Borough Council and Barrow Borough Transport. Arising from this, the prospective purchaser refused to exchange contracts.

With no purchaser now coming forward, Barrow Borough Transport ceased to trade at 15.30 hours on 26th May 1989 with buses being withdrawn at just 2 hours notice. Ribble, it seemed, had won the battle but there was another interesting development to come as we shall see in the next chapter. The depot and 24 vehicles were taken over by Ribble but they made a point of not operating any vehicles in Barrow whilst still in Barrow livery. As a result of this, vehicles in Barrow livery could be seen operating in other parts of Ribble territory. A further effect was that a number of Cumberland vehicles arrived in Barrow in late May to assist Ribble whilst former Barrow vehicles were away for repaint.

A RIBBLE PERSPECTIVE ON BARROW

During 1985 and the early part of 1986 there was a flurry of activity in bus planning offices across the UK. As mentioned in the previous chapter, the Transport Act 1985 had just become Statute and in addition to the privatisation of the National Bus Company, which included Ribble, there was also the deregulation of bus services, which all needed dealing with.

In order to allow Local Authorities to identify gaps in any new commercial network from 26th October 1986, all Operators had to register all bus services they felt could be operated commercially, *ie* at a profit, by the end of February 1986, ready to start in October 1986.

Ribble had decided to expand its network into Barrow from its base at Ulverston by opening up a low cost depot in Barrow and running minibuses linking the town centre with a number of areas and estates in the town. This was in addition to the services that it had operated for 50 years or more in and out of Barrow.

During the course of 1985 timetables were developed and routes firmed up.

The area team based at Kendal had managed to borrow a Mercedes 608D minibus from sister company East Midlands Motor Services and that was utilised running around Barrow, pathfinding carefully selecting routes that would make Ribble's *mini*link network more attractive by penetrating the larger estates within Barrow.

Ribble borrowed Mercedes 608D minibus, C901 HWF, from East Midlands Motor Services to carry out route testing around estates in Barrow prior to introducing their '*mini*link' services. *(SB)*

Ribble Motor Services – Routes Registered in Barrow for Deregulation

B1	Ocean Road Walney, Town Centre, Ormsgill	Mondays – Saturdays
B2	Middle Hill, Newbarns, Town Centre, Furness Hospital	Mondays – Saturdays
B3	West Shore Walney, Town Centre	1 early am working
B4	Holbeck, Town Centre, North Scale	Sunday afternoons
B4	Town Centre, North Scale	Mon-Fri Early am

Needless to say, when the details of Ribble's new services in Barrow were published by the Traffic Commissioner, the Local Authority and other pressure groups were up in arms. Historically, Barrow Corporation Transport buses had remained on the main roads and intending passengers walked to the bus stop.

Ribble *mini*link had this strange concept of penetrating the housing estates and in a lot of cases would operate a hail and ride system picking up people outside their houses. The Ribble timetable also offered high frequencies with buses every 10 minutes between Walney into the town centre and Ormsgill (Service B1) with Service B2 providing similar level of services between Newbarns and Barrow and on to Furness General Hospital. The services would operate from before 07.00 right through until early evening with evening services

offering departures every 20 minutes until after 23.00. Indeed, the *mini*link network was marketed as being fast, frequent and friendly.

As 1986 progressed the Traffic Commissioner for the North West held an enquiry into Ribble *mini*link's proposed routes in Barrow. There had been some objections raised by Local Authorities and pressure groups regarding the proposed routes which could have removed the minibuses from the side streets and kept them to the main roads. Evidence on both sides was put forward at a noisy public enquiry and at the end the Traffic Commissioner ruled that the majority of the proposed routes around Hawcoat, Newbarns, Walney and Ormsgill were more than suitable for use by minibuses. However, a couple of streets had traffic regulation orders placed on them which prohibited use by buses but there were plenty of other suitable alternatives and Ribble plans continued apace.

During the course of the summer premises were obtained at Emlyn Street. This was a very small base that was rented to start the network. It had been previously utilised as a car hire depot. It would just fit 12 vehicles with a very small office, acting as a staff mess area, office and driver's room.

Staff recruitment also started with interviews being held at the Ribble-owned National Travel World travel agency on Dalton Road. Virtually all the new drivers recruited were new into the industry and were recruited for their customer care strengths rather than having a PCV licence. In those days a 'minibus only' bus licence was the requirement and because the same technique as driving a van

sufficed, then training was shorter and easier than a large bus training programme.

Ribble in Barrow also won some early morning and Sunday tender workings and without much fanfare the first Ribble *mini*link service rolled out of Emlyn Street and onto the streets of Barrow on Sunday 26th October 1986 when a tendered service between Barrow town centre and Holbeck was started. The first commercial services started the following day on the Monday morning. The fleet was primarily Mercedes 608D, with a mixture of 19 and-20 seaters. The 19-seaters were high back "coach seated" and the 20-seaters were the bus seated version. There was even a scattering of 16-seater Freight Rover Sherpa minibuses utilised too. These had a Dormobile body and were not all that well received by staff or passengers.

Any fears that people of Barrow would resist the *mini*link revolution were immediately proven unfounded as the popularity of these services exceeded all expectations. The high frequency Minibus service was here to stay.

Further services were altered in January 1987. This was the first time that bus operators could amend their licences and the bus timetables they had been operating since October 1986. The opportunity was taken to introduce even more services into Barrow including the West Shore area of Walney and a Monday to Saturday high frequency service between the town centre and Holbeck.

An urgent search was now underway for new

Typifying Ribble operations, Mercedes 608D minibus No. 522 negotiates Ramsden Square heading for South Walney. *(HP)*

Operating on service B1 to South Walney on 14th June 1989, Ribble Mercedes 608D minibus No. 519 travels along Abbey Road past the railway station. *(HP)*

larger premises but in the end Emlyn Street was kept as the operating base, with parking space for some Minibuses, and with the overflow being parked overnight at a local haulier's yard. Regular maintenance and cleaning took place at Emlyn Street with the mother depot at Ulverston taking on more major jobs.

As the months and years progressed Ribble *mini*link became embedded into Barrow. Whilst Barrow Transport tried to counter by expanding their network to Ulverston and Kendal and within Kendal, Ribble concentrated on improving and refining its timetables within Barrow, where the majority of passengers were.

Ribble Leyland National B type No. 807 operating on service B4 to Holbeck Farm is shown in Ramsden Square. It is carrying the '*mini*link' name under the fleet name at the front. *(HP)*

In March 1988 Ribble was finally bought from the National Bus Company by its management team. There were two competing management teams to buy the Company but the A team was the successful bidder in the end. One of their early acquisitions was the Preston-based Zippy Minibus fleet that had been set up a year earlier by United Transport.

When it was heard in advance that Barrow Transport were obtaining some Talbot Pullman Minibuses to convert some of their services, Ribble overnight transferred eight tri-axle Talbot Pullmans from Zippy at Preston into Barrow to replace a mixture of Mercedes 608Ds and Freight Rover Sherpas.

During 1988 the financial situation at Barrow Transport became public knowledge and it came as no surprise when Administrators were appointed to keep the business going whilst possible purchasers were sought.

During the course of late 1988 and 1989 it was expected that eventually Barrow Transport would cease trading or be bought out by another operator.

Emergency timetables and crew schedules had been produced in preparation, so from March 1989 everything was ready...........just in case.

Ribble Talbot minibus 072 draws up at the Town Hall heading for North Scale with a similar vehicle in the background on 5th October 1988. *(HP)*

Travelling along Abbey Road and passing the railway station on 14th June 1989 is Ribble Leyland National B type No. 803 displaying the *mini*link name at the front. *(HP)*

When news came of Barrow Transport cessation of operations on 26th May 1989 Ribble was able to bring in reserve buses and staff to operate an enlarged network in the town with frequencies as high as every 7/8 minutes.

Further away from Barrow, yet another interesting development had taken place with effect from Friday 21st April 1989 when Ribble Motor Services was again taken over, by Stagecoach. This was to have a significant effect on Barrow as we shall see in the next chapter.

Whilst there are arguments for and against de-regulation, certainly the people of Barrow gained from having competition in their town. The end result was that they finished up with a high frequency local bus network that continues to this day under the Stagecoach in Cumbria and North Lancashire umbrella.

Park Royal-bodied Leyland Atlantean No. 1383 in the Ribble fleet passes the railway station as it travels along Abbey Road towards the town centre on 14th June 1989. The cyclist appears to be viewing the photographer with suspicion. *(HP)*

CUMBERLAND IN BARROW

Reference was made in the previous chapter to the fact that Ribble Motor Services had been taken over by Stagecoach with effect from Friday 21st April 1989 and arising from this the new owner decided that the operations of Ribble in South Lakeland and the Furness area should be transferred to another subsidiary, namely Cumberland Motor Services based, at that time, in Whitehaven. Included in the Cumberland takeover were depots at Barrow, Ulverston and Kendal, together with the respective out-stations at Grange over Sands, Ambleside, Sedbergh and Appleby.

This transfer took effect from 18th June 1989 meaning that Ribble, having fought hard to win the battle for Barrow, lost it within a month. As a further result of this, Cumberland Motor Services became the major operator throughout the County of Cumbria. Prior to this the only input which Cumberland had into Barrow was the operation of a number of express services on behalf of National Express, these being operated from Whitehaven depot with the vehicles returning to Whitehaven once per week for servicing.

With the change of control between the two Stagecoach companies, the local management structure changed with Ribble's area office in Kendal closing. Tony Cox took up the position of Traffic Manager with United Counties in Northampton, another Stagecoach company, and Stephie Barber, who had been involved in the development of Ribble activities in the Furness area in the 1980s, became local manager at Barrow. Trevor Pennington moved from Lancaster to become local manager at Kendal.

Ribble had purchased the depot and 24 vehicles as detailed in the **'Schedule of Vehicles Taken Over by Ribble Motor Services'** (Appendix 3) but there was a policy of not operating in Barrow vehicles in the Barrow livery of blue and cream. Two Leyland Nationals, Nos. 16 and 17, were delivered to Whitehaven for painting into Stagecoach livery whilst Nos. 11, 15, 20–23 were painted by Ribble at Preston. Some Leyland Nationals, including No. 13, and the Leyland Atlanteans were used by Ribble from Preston, still in Barrow livery, but with Ribble fleetnames applied. Cumberland sent Leyland Nationals Nos. 351, 353, 357, 369 and 811 to Barrow to help out. All except 357 had their Cumberland fleetnames removed although 811 had not, at that time, received fleetnames following a repaint.

One of the first ex-Barrow vehicles to be painted into Stagecoach livery was Leyland National 2 No. 22 and as a result it received Ribble fleetnames. It became No 897 and when photographed in Duke Street in July 1989 had become part of the Cumberland fleet and received Cumberland legal lettering. *(HP)*

Eastern Coach Works-bodied Leyland Atlantean No. 1410 parked at the Town Hall in July 1989 was displaying Ribble fleetnames but was by then a Cumberland vehicle and displayed Cumberland legal lettering. *(HP)*

Repainted Barrow Leyland Nationals received Cumberland fleetnames with the exception of No. 760, ex-Barrow No. 15, and No. 897, ex-Barrow 22, which received Ribble fleetnames, having been repainted prior to the change from Ribble to Cumberland being announced. With the return of the former Barrow vehicles to Barrow, the Cumberland Nationals returned to Whitehaven where they were prepared for the journey north to Perth to join the fleet of Perth Panthers. If a

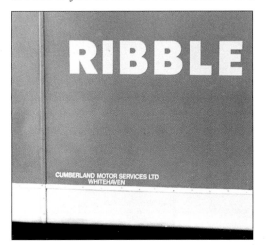

Barrow-based vehicle had to go to Whitehaven for any reason, it would invariably return with the Ribble fleetname replaced by a Cumberland fleetname. Similar changes were carried out at Barrow, Ulverston and Kendal.

When it was decided that Cumberland should take over, some further change of vehicles took place in that Park Royal-bodied Leyland Atlanteans were transferred to other Ribble depots and replaced with Eastern Coach Works-bodied examples similar to those inherited by Cumberland from Ribble with the Carlisle and Penrith depots. Legal lettering on vehicles had to be changed for the date of takeover but most vehicles retained their Ribble fleetnames initially, giving rise to the unusual situation of vehicles carrying Ribble fleetnames but Cumberland legal lettering.

When the operations in Barrow passed from Ribble to Cumberland, legal lettering had to be changed immediately and this created the unusual situation of vehicles carrying Ribble fleetnames and Cumberland Motor Service legal lettering. *(HP)*

At this time, Cumberland Motor Services, despite being part of the Stagecoach Group, was still trading as 'CMS Cumberland', a style adopted in the run-up to privatisation and making use of the long established **CMS** abbreviation by which the Company had been generally known in its traditional area of West Cumberland. Accordingly, early publicity material and correspondence was conducted under this heading.

A set of five timetable leaflets in *CMS Cumberland* style was issued to take effect from 22nd July 1989 covering Barrow Town Services as follows :-

1.	**B1 Minibus** South Walney, Amphitrite Street, Coffee House, Town Hall, Oxford Street, Hawcoat Estate, Furness General Hospital
	B7 Minibus Biggar Bank, South Walney, Amphitrite Street, Coffee House, Town Hall, Oxford Street, Hawcoat Estate , Furness General Hospital
2.	**B2** West Shore, Coffee House, Town Hall, Ormsgill
3.	**B3** Town Hall, Washington Hotel, Newbarns
4.	**B4** Town Hall, Greengate Street, Washington Hotel, Holbeck Farm
	B14 Minibus Town Hall, Greengate Street, Washington Hotel, Holbeck Farm, Roose
5.	**B5** Town Hall, Coffee House, Tea House, Vickerstown, North Scale
	B15 Minibus Town Hall, Blake Street

	The following school journeys were also detailed on these leaflets.
1	**B22** Biggar Bank, Abbey Road, St Bernards and return
2	**B24** St Bernards, West Shore
	B28 Ocean Road Walney Comprehensive School, West Shore
4	**B25** Holbeck Farm, Washington Hotel, St Bernards and return
5	**B23** North Scale, Washington Hotel, St Bernards and return

In 1989 Cumberland purchased three new Leyland Lynx models, the locally built replacement for the Leyland National, together with an ex-demonstrator. These vehicles were allocated to Barrow, being the first full size new single-deck vehicles for the town since the Leyland National 2 models in 1980. In 1991, a further example was purchased from Ribble.

As former Barrow vehicles returned from repaint at either Preston or Whitehaven, the fleet settled down and the CMS Allocation Schedule for August 1989 showed the following vehicles allocated to Barrow.

Leyland Atlantean AN68 Nos. 1407, 1410, 1411, 1413, 1415, 1417, 1426.

Leyland National B type No. 803.

Leyland National 1 Nos. 446, 716, 755, 757, 758, 760, 761, 762, 3781.

Leyland National 2 Nos. 857, 895, 896, 897, 898.

Former Ribble Talbot minibus No. 076, now part of the Cumberland fleet, was still displaying '*mini*link' livery when photographed at the Town Hall in July 1989. *(HP)*

The Alexander bodied Mercedes 709 minibus was not a very elegant vehicle but it was soundly constructed, being coachbuilt rather than a van conversion. Photographed at the Town Hall is No. 48, one of the first of the type allocated to Cumberland and originally based at Whitehaven. *(HP)*

Cumberland purchased four new Leyland Lynx and allocated them to Barrow. They were numbered 251-254 and the first of these is shown at the Town Hall on 7th September 1989 awaiting departure to West Shore. *(HP)*

Leyland Lynx Nos. 251-254.
Mercedes 608 Minibus Nos. 533, 559, 561.
Peugeot Express Minibus Nos. 70-79 (All ex-Ribble).

The Peugeot Talbot Express minibuses were to have very short lives with Cumberland and had been withdrawn by the time that the September allocation schedule was issued. They were replaced by six Mercedes 608 models numbered 33-38, transferred from Whitehaven depot and also four similar vehicles ex-Ribble and numbered 518, 519, 522 and 562.

Three examples of the Stagecoach standard Mercedes 709 minibuses with Alexander coachbuilt bodies, as distinct from the van conversion bodies on the 608 models, arrived in early 1990. Further examples followed and these vehicles figured prominently in Barrow services in the succeeding years.

In February 1990 Ulverston depot, based at The Ellers, was closed with all operations transferred to the depot at Hindpool Road, Barrow, although a small number of vehicles were out-stationed at the local Mercedes garage with one vehicle parked out at Coniston and another at Haverthwaite. The Ulverston site, which had housed the Ribble

Former Bluebird Buses Alexander-bodied Leyland Olympian No. 1090 is shown at the Town Hall awaiting departure to West Shore and illustrating the use of a coloured destination blind which had been a Barrow tradition since 1934. *(HP)*

With the Town Hall clock prominent in the background, Alexander-bodied Volvo B10M No. 762 heads along Michaelson Road Bridge to West Shore on service 2. *(HP)*

depot since 1932, was developed as premises for the local Ford agent.

Five Alexander-bodied Leyland Olympians were purchased from another Stagecoach subsidiary, Bluebird Buses Limited, Aberdeen, and were allocated to Barrow. The first three arrived in December 1991 and were unusual in that they had been re-registered with earlier registration numbers, GSO 3-5V in place of the original C473/4 XRS and D375 XRS when new in 1986 and 1987. These were subsequently re-registered by Cumberland as C382/3 SAO and D384 XAO to reflect their true age. The other two vehicles had their original registration numbers, D380/1 XRS, and arrived in February 1992.

March 1993 saw the biggest single investment in public transport in Barrow since the arrival of the Leyland PD2 double-deck vehicles in the years 1949-51. A fleet of 22 Volvo B10M single-deck buses with Alexander bodies was launched by the then MP for Barrow Mr John Hutton. An investment of this size was driven by the need to drastically reduce engineering costs by having a large part of the fleet utilising new buses. The vehicles were part of a large order placed by Cumberland which had originally been intended to comprise 100 Volvo B6 single-deckers of lighter construction. The order was changed following dissatisfaction with the first batch of B6 vehicles delivered to the company and was finalised as 92 Volvo B10Ms for Cumberland with the remaining eight going elsewhere in the Stagecoach Group. It was a change for which the local management was thankful. At the launch of these vehicles it was announced that an investment of £500,000 was to be made in a new depot to replace the Hindpool Road premises.

The premises in Hindpool Road were in very poor condition suffering from lack of investment over the years, with a leaking roof and poorly maintained building fabric. In the winter of 1994/95 the building suffered extensive roof damage in gales. New accommodation was found by taking over part of the building and yard at the

A view of the front of Hindpool Road Depot in August 1991 with Megadecker 1202, Duple Dominant 2-bodied coach No. 625, Leyland National B types Nos. 803 and 207. *(HP)*

The East Lancashire Coachbuilders Dennis Tridents provided by Cumbria County Council for the X35 service were launched at Haverthwaite railway station forecourt on 28th February 2006. *(HP)*

premises of R Brady and Sons Limited, Haulage Contractors in Walney Road. The yard area was developed for bus parking and the building was converted to provide workshop and office accommodation. The move to the new depot took place over the weekend of 23rd/24th April 1995

with the official opening taking place on Friday 12th May 1995 performed by John Hutton MP in the presence of Anne Gloag, joint founder of Stagecoach, and Les Warneford, Managing Director of Stagecoach Cumberland at that time.

The fleet at this time comprised 14 double-

Optare Solo No. 47135 displays the 'Network Barrow' signage at the front and side as it picks up passengers in Abbey Road *en route* to the hospital. *(HP)*

deck, 14 single-deck and 23 minibuses. This total included buses based at Millom which had previously been an out-station of Whitehaven but now came under the day to day control of Barrow, and also vehicles out-stationed at Ulverston, Askam and Haverthwaite. It had been some nine years since the introduction of minibuses into Barrow but they were still proving very popular linking the town centre with surrounding estates.

Following this were years of consolidation and development of the network in Barrow. Service X35 was established as a twice weekly shopping link from Kendal to Barrow following development of the Portland Walk Shopping Centre in Barrow. It soon became apparent that the real demand was from Barrow to Kendal and a regular limited stop service between the two towns commenced in 1997 and was an immediate success. It connected with a four routes rural network at Ulverston providing a link to and from Kendal with Broughton, Coniston and two rural routes from Barrow to Ulverston.

This rural network was supported by Cumbria County Council with the result that they became more involved with the X35 service and provided three new double-deckers for the purpose. They were Dennis Tridents with bodies by East Lancashire Coachbuilders and carried Cumberland Motor Services legal lettering. They were the first new East Lancashire-bodied vehicles to carry Cumberland legal lettering since the Leyland TD7 models of 1941. Officially launched at Haverthwaite Railway Station forecourt on 28th February 2006, they were limited to operation on this service and because of this required very limited destination displays being fitted with destination blinds, rather than electronically operated. All three buses were unreliable, being unsuited to the nature of high speed inter-urban work. It was also considered that the dark blue livery did not make the best impression with customers. The service continued in operation until 2nd September 2012.

The contract became due for re-tender and Stagecoach was unsuccessful. Rather than surrender the route which it had developed from its start in 1997, Stagecoach decided to operate the service commercially. It was therefore replaced by a new service X6 which commenced operation on 3rd September 2012 using new Scania E400 double-deckers with ADL bodies to the Stagecoach standard specification. Two existing similar double-deckers, featuring high back coach style seating were transferred from Kendal depot.

The Alexander-bodied Mercedes 709 minibuses were replaced in 2005 by Optare Solo minibuses seating 27, a vehicle designed from the start as a minibus rather than being an adaptation of a commercial vehicle and one which had proved very popular throughout the country. It is an interesting fact that although classed as a minibus, these vehicles are of similar length and are in fact wider than the traditional front-engined rear-entrance double-decker.

Local identity for Town Services was introduced with these vehicles using the name 'Network Barrow'. This name has, however, now been dropped and replaced by the slogan 'Love Barrow'. In 2008 a number of these vehicles had names applied relating to ships built in the local shipyard and one, No. 47147, received a special overall livery marking Barrow's long association with the shipbuilding industry.

At the end of 2012 the fleet allocated to Barrow was a very modern one comprising 34 vehicles of which 31 are of the low floor easy access type. This total is made up of 19 Optare Solo single-deckers, seven Scania double-deckers with Alexander bodies, five Dennis Trident double-deckers with Alexander bodies and three Volvo Olympian double-deckers with Alexander bodies.

With a modern fleet and well equipped up-to-date maintenance premises the Company is in a position to continue serving the people of Barrow and the Furness Peninsula for years to come.

TRAM PICTORIAL

Sometimes things go wrong! Here, a steam tram locomotive has become derailed in the Strand, almost certainly due to the poor state of the track. *(IC/KNC)*

A view of an unidentified steam tram locomotive and trailer with crew. *(GHC)*

An early view looking up Abbey Road from Ramsden Square with a steam tram. Also visible is the passing loop in the track at this point. *(REC)*

Abbey Road, Barrow-in-Furness

Photographed with its crew at Abbey Terminus is BET car No 5, one of the original trams delivered to Barrow in February 1904 for the commencement of electric operation. *(STA)*

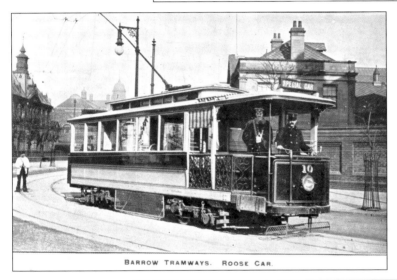

BARROW TRAMWAYS.   ROOSE CAR.

Entering Ramsden Square from Abbey Road is tram No 10. This was one of five, numbered 8-12, purchased in 1904 for the Roose service where single-deckers were required in order to pass beneath the Salthouse Road railway bridge. *(GHC)*

Schneider Square with demi-car tram No 13. The addition of roof board adverts changes its appearance quite considerably. *(IC/KN)*

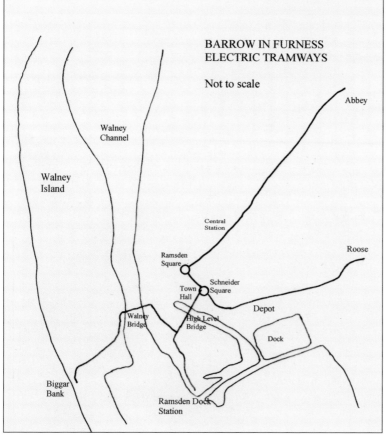

BARROW IN FURNESS
ELECTRIC TRAMWAYS

Not to scale

Abbey

Walney
Channel

Walney
Island

Central
Station

Roose

Ramsden
Square

Schneider
Square

Town
Hall

Depot

Walney
Bridge

High Level
Bridge

Dock

Biggar
Bank

Ramsden Dock
Station

Two Brush Conaty double-deck cars were purchased in 1905 and numbered 15 and 16. Both are shown here with No. 16 to the front at Ramsden Dock Station with crew. The long wheelbase four-wheel truck is clearly visible. Once again we have a young lady and child.*(STA)*

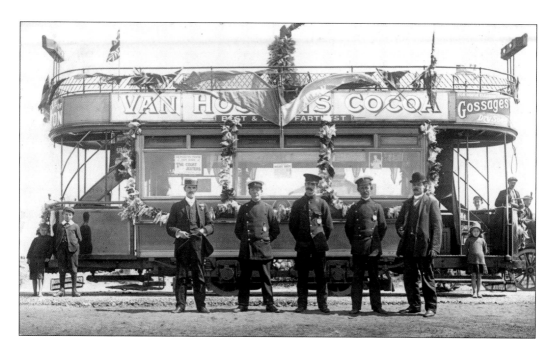

The tramway to Biggar Bank on Walney Island was opened on 4th August 1911 and this was one of a number of views taken to commemorate the event. *(GHC/Ckn)*

Brush Conaty car No. 16 with a good selection of people posing for the photographer, and an interesting range of food and drink being advertised. *(IC/KN)*

A view on the High Level Bridge at going home time from the Shipyard with a well loaded tram and many walking. *(GHC)*

One of four double-deck cars numbered 17-20 and seating 96 passengers, tram No. 17 loads in Schneider Square displaying the destination 'Tea House'. *(GHC/HAW)*

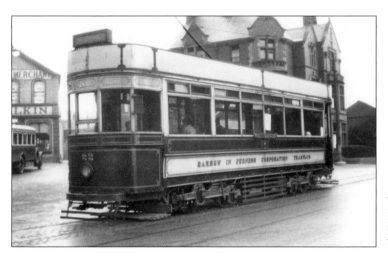

Tram No. 22 crosses Schneider Square with an unidentified single-deck bus in the background. *(GHC/HAW)*

Another view of the High Level Bridge with a mass exodus from the Shipyard and a tram making little progress as it is surrounded by the crowds. *(GHC/Ckn)*

An unidentified double-deck tram crosses Walney Bridge and arrives on Walney Island. *(GHC)*

An early view of Ramsden Square with one of the first four open-top trams. *(GHC/ Ckn)*

BARROW-IN-FURNESS,RAMSDEN SQUARE, AND DUKE STREET

Brush car No. 22 was one of four numbered 21-4 delivered to BET in 1913 with seats for 40 passengers. It is shown here with its crew. In 1920 car 24 was re-built by Glasgow Corporation at the Coplaw Hill Works along with two sets of maximum traction bogies in what is believed to have been a unique exercise for Barrow. It reflected the condition of the former BET fleet at the time the corporation took over, the latter having insufficient resources for such essential major re-building projects. *(TLP)*

A view inside the Brush works at Loughborough with Barrow Corporation trams Nos. 41 and 45 under construction in 1921. These were part of a batch numbered 35-46 and were the only new tramcars to be purchased by Barrow Corporation. *(KNC)*

Brush single-deck tram No. 40 at the Abbey Road terminus. The Corporation's coat-of-arms will be noted, as will be the lack of roof board adverts. *(GHC)*

The end of an era and the beginning of a new one. Crowds gather to welcome the Crossley double-deck buses on 5th April 1932 as they take over from the trams. *(EM)*

On the last day of tramway operation 5th April 1932 the official party is shown about to board the tram. *(EM)*

Officials gather with Tram No. 45 on 5th April 1932, the floral wreath marking the last day of tramway operation. *(EM)*

THE FIRST BUSES - BET

Daimler charabanc EO 579, delivered to BET in Barrow in 1914, was later transferred to Sheerness, but by the time of this photograph it was owned by the Potteries Electric Tramway Company, still in the BET empire. *(STA)*

British Electric Traction Ltd purchased four Daimler CD models in 1914 and one of these, EO 577, is illustrated here. *(EM)*

Illustrated with its proud crew is EO 757, a Daimler CD type with Birch body dating from 1914. *(PCC)*

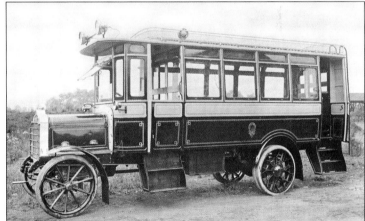

The body design on the Daimler CD chassis was a BET standard and these views taken at the Brush works prior to the First World War show how neat and attractive they were when new. This vehicle would enter service with the Potteries company. *(STA both)*

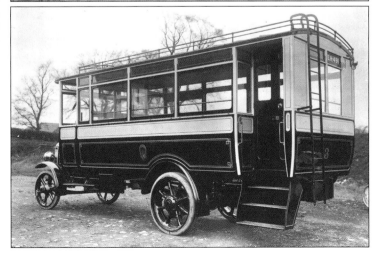

Two early unidentified vehicles are shown outside the Jute Works on Abbey Road. *(GHC)*

BARROW BUSES

Shown earlier, but repeated here to allow comparison, in the early days Barrow Corporation operated a number of Guy B type single-deckers and this one, EO 3463 carried fleet number 1. It was on loan from Guy Motors pending delivery of Nos 2-5 which arrived later in 1925. *(RMC)*

This vehicle was one of two Guy-bodied Guy B type supplied in 1928, and numbered 1 and 2. This one was number 2, and both were withdrawn in December 1932. *(RMC)*

Leyland double-deckers first made an appearance in the Barrow fleet in 1929 when four TD1 models with Leyland open staircase bodies arrived numbered 15-8. Photographed when new were Nos. 15 and 16 shown here. *(TLP)*

A prewar view of the High Level Bridge with a Leyland TD1 leading a line of buses facing the camera as workers leave the Shipyard. *(GHC)*

Photographed at Ulverston, awaiting return to Barrow is 1931 Leyland TS3 fleet No. 9 with Leyland body. Standing behind is a Leyland Cheetah, a lighter weight model of a type which was well represented in the fleet of its owner, Ribble Motor Services. *(AEJC)*

A Crossley advert publicising the replacement of Barrow trams by Crossley double-deck buses. *(STA)*

This photograph showing the Town Hall and Schneider Square probably dates from the mid thirties. In the foreground is petrol-engined Crossley Condor No. 36, one of nine purchased along with nine diesel-engined examples for tramway replacement in 1932. All had bodies by Northern Counties. *(GHC)*

A rear view of English Electric lowbridge-bodied Leyland TD4c No. 28, dating from 1937, as it makes its way along the Promenade on Walney Island. *(GHC)*

Photographed for the body builders when new is English Electric-bodied Leyland TD4c No. 24. It was one of four delivered in 1936. *(REC)*

In years gone by Leyland Motors regularly sent out photographers to record vehicles in service. Here the subject is 1936 TD4c No. 24 with its English Electric highbridge body at the Town Hall stop. *(STA)*

Lowbridge double-deckers were required for operation under Salthouse Road Bridge and a Leyland TD4c model numbered 28, with English Electric body, was purchased in 1937 along with two TD5c examples also with English Electric bodies numbered 29/30. Photographed when new is No. 28. *(EEC/REC)*

Photographed for the makers when new is 1939 Leyland TD5c with English Electric highbridge body, fleet No. 61. It was one of six similar vehicles. *(STA)*

An interesting view showing English Electric-bodied Leyland TD4c No. 27 dating from 1936 with the docks and the ship 'Stratheden' in the background. *(STA)*

In 1943 a number of prewar single-deckers were re-bodied by East Lancashire Coachbuilders as illustrated by No. 4 shown here in 1953. The Leyland TS4 chassis dated from 1933 and the vehicle remained in service until December 1955. Most rebodying of single-deckers in the wartime period was carried out by HV Burlingham of Blackpool and these bodies are similar in outline to the Burlingham examples. The main difference is the provision of window pans brought about by the continued use of metal framework by East Lancashire Coachbuilders. *(RM)*

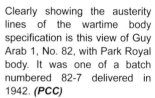

Clearly showing the austerity lines of the wartime body specification is this view of Guy Arab 1, No. 82, with Park Royal body. It was one of a batch numbered 82-7 delivered in 1942. *(PCC)*

Also photographed when new at Park Royal, this rear view indicates the unglazed rear upstairs window, a feature which was part of the wartime body specification. *(GHC)*

Clearly indicating the problems created by the snow in the winter of 1940/41 is this view taken of a double-decker stranded on the Coast Road with staff endeavouring to release it. There was a second double-decker some yards behind this one. *(PCC)*

It must have been very hard work clearing snow of this depth and extent with shovels. Despite this these hardy men managed a smile for the photographer. *(PCC)*

PEACETIME DELIVERIES RESUME

When the first batch of postwar Crossleys was received in May 1948, No. 42 was paraded at the Town Hall to allow the public to see the new vehicles. The reason for the raised waistrail level in the last two windows of the lower and upper saloon is that the vehicles did not have chassis extensions and the staircase and platform were cantilevered from the body structure. Additional framing for this purpose was incorporated at upper saloon level and the lower saloon windows were made to match. *(HPC)*

A postwar view in the workshops at Hindpool Road depot as Crossley and Leyland vehicles receive attention. *(GHC)*

Crossley-bodied Crossley No. 102 was one of the second batch of Crossley double-deckers supplied in 1948 and is shown here in 1953 with a Park Royal-bodied Leyland PD2 in the background. *(RM)*

Nearest the camera is Crossley-bodied Crossley No. 49 from the first batch of ten received in 1948. Alongside is Park Royal-bodied Leyland PD2 No. 151 dating from 1951 and beyond that Park Royal-bodied Leyland PD2 No. 121 dating from 1949. *(PN)*

Photographed at handover are two of the 30 Park Royal-bodied Leyland PD2s delivered in 1949 with No. 132 at the front and No. 131 behind. Mr Thomas Lord, the Barrow General Manager, is at the right of the group and Robert Gregg, Park Royal Contracts Manager, is at the left. *(STA)*

With 30 examples delivered in the year 1949, Park Royal-bodied Leyland PD2s soon dominated the bus scene in Barrow and No. 138 from this batch presents a familiar scene in the town operating on this Circular service. *(TLP)*

Leyland TD4c No. 14 dating from 1937 was converted into a breakdown truck in 1949. It is shown strategically posed with the depot in the background. *(STA)*

With its progress impeded by cyclists and pedestrians, one of the Park Royal-bodied Leyland PD2s makes its way at the High Level Bridge as workers exit the Shipyard. Another example of a similar vehicle is in the background. A familiar site in Barrow over many years. *(EM)*

In 1950 a further ten Park Royal-bodied Leyland PD2s arrived numbered 141-50 and No. 148 is shown here in service. The complete batch was re-bodied by Chas H Roe in 1959/60 *(HPC)*

The first underfloor-engined single-deckers to be received by Barrow were two Leyland-bodied Leyland Royal Tigers delivered in 1952 and numbered 50/1. The first of these is shown at the depot. *(RM)*

The second of the pair of Royal Tigers was later converted by the Department into a travelling library. When a third Royal Tiger was required, Leyland had ceased building bus bodies and the contract went to Massey Bros in Pemberton, as seen opposite. *(STA)*

Number 52, photographed at Massey's factory, shows the neat design and clean lines. It also featured in advertising from Young Window manufacturers, as seen below. *(STA both)*

The Park Royal-bodied Leyland PD2s delivered in 1958 were to a later body design and this is clearly shown in this view of No. 161, the first of the ten which were numbered 161-70. *(TLP)*

Leyland PD2 No. 149 dating from 1950 is shown after being re-bodied by Chas Roe in 1959. The distinctive patent waistrail, a traditional Roe feature, can be discerned below the lower deck window line. *(TLP)*

Leyland PD2 No. 2, with bodywork by Massey, picks up passengers in Duke Street on 27th July 1965. In 1970 it was renumbered 102. *(VTP)*

Displaying the later livery, No. 102, is shown in Ramsden Square in July 1972. *(RD)*

The 1967 Leyland Leopards had East Lancashire Coachbuilders bodies, albeit built by their associate company, Neepsend Coachworks in Sheffield. They were numbered 55-9 and No. 56 was photographed crossing the railway bridge on Abbey Road with the station sign in the background on 14th August 1986. It was still looking presentable despite being 19 years old. *(HP)*

Having emerged from Duke Street, Leyland Leopard No. 62 dating from 1968, negotiates the roundabout in Ramsden Square *en route* to Abbey on 6th July 1972. In the background is a Massey- bodied Leyland PD2. *(RD)*

Shown entering Duke Street from Ramsden Square on 9th April 1977 is East Lancashire-bodied Leyland Leopard No. 45, heading for the Town Hall and North Scale. *(RD)*

Picking up passengers at the Town Hall stop on 14th August 1986 is East Lancashire-bodied Daimler Fleetline, No. 4, operating to Biggar Bank. *(HP)*

Parked in Ulverston on 6th July 1972 is Daimler Fleetline No. 4 again, with similar vehicle No. 1 parked behind. *(RD)*

Photographed at Southport on 19th August 1976 is Duple-bodied Bedford VAL 70 coach DTJ 633J, one of ten coaches taken over with the business of Hadwin's Coaches and numbered H10 in the Barrow Fleet. All the coaches taken over were Bedford VAL models with Duple bodies. *(RD)*

The Leyland National was an integral vehicle, without separate chassis designed between Leyland and the National Bus Company and assembled in a purpose-built factory at Lillyhall in West Cumberland. Barrow purchased 5 in 1974, numbered 6-10 and No. 7 was photographed at the Town Hall in March 1974 a month after entering service and still gleaming in its fresh paintwork. *(MB)*

Photographed at Walney Island on 14th August 1986 is Leyland National No. 7 dating from 1974. *(HP)*

Leyland National No. 14, dating from 1977, leaves Ulverston for Barrow Ramsden Square on 25th March 1978 with two Ribble single-deckers in the background. *(RD)*

In the scenic setting of Walney Promenade, Leyland National No. 8 heads for the Town Hall on 14th August 1986. The location is very close to that in which the Leyland TD4c double-decker was photographed about 50 years previously and shown on page 64 *(HP)*

Leyland National No. 12 heads along Michaelson Road towards the high level bridge on 27th September 1979 *en route* to Biggar Bank on Walney Island. *(RD)*

The original Leyland National, generally referred to as the Leyland National 1, was replaced by the Leyland National 2 which was a much improved vehicle. The unsatisfactory 500 series engine was replaced by the well established 680 series used by Leyland for some years in other buses. Barrow purchased four of the revised models in 1980, numbered 20-3 and No. 22 was photographed on the Coast Road heading for Ulverston on 13th March 1985. *(HP)*

Dissatisfaction with the Leyland National, particularly the 500 series engine which had been developed by Leyland for this vehicle, led to the purchase in 1979 of two Dennis Dominators with East Lancashire Coachbuilders bodies. Like the Daimler Fleetline, the Dennis Dominator was basically a double-deck chassis but a number were supplied for single-deck bodies. The chassis had been developed originally to meet the needs of a particular operator who was dissatisfied with the limited range which Leyland was prepared to offer. One of the two, No. 18, is shown in Abbey Road on 10th April 1985. *(HP)*

After a short period with no double-decks in the fleet, Barrow purchased three DMS Leyland Fleetline double-deckers ex-London Transport and numbered them 101-3. One of these, No. 101, was photographed in August 1985 passing over the railway bridge in Abbey Road with one of the trusty Leyland Leopards travelling in the opposite direction. *(HP)*

Ex-London Transport Leyland Fleetline No. 109 is shown on Abbey Road heading out of town to Abbey in July 1984. *(HP)*

The first new double-deckers to be purchased by Barrow since the Massey-bodied Leyland PD2s in 1961 arrived in 1983 and comprised three Leyland Atlantean AN68D/1R models with Northern Counties bodies numbered 104-6. Shown in Abbey Road on 10th April 1985 is No. 105. *(HP)*

Heading along Duke Street for the Shipyard on 14th August 1986 is Leyland Atlantean No. 106. *(HP)*

BARROW BOROUGH TRANSPORT LIMITED

Showing the large 'BBT' vinyl applied to existing vehicles on the takeover by Barrow Borough Transport Limited, is East Lancashire-bodied Leyland Leopard, No. 49, as it heads down Abbey Road on 19th April 1987. *(HP)*

Showing the position of the 'BBT' vinyls as applied to the offside of Leyland Nationals is No. 12 at the Town Hall awaiting departure to Holbeck Farm. *(RD)*

Leyland Atlantean No. 105, loading at the Town Hall, illustrates the position of the 'BBT' Vinyls on double-deck vehicles still in the Barrow Corporation livery. *(RD)*

Barrow Borough Transport Ltd purchased three used Leyland Atlanteans, two of which had Park Royal bodies and had originally been in the fleet of Plymouth City Transport. They were numbered 101/2 and the latter is shown in Schneider Square heading for the Shipyard. *(RM)*

The third used Atlantean was numbered 103 and carried an Alexander body. It came from Delaine of Bourne but had originally been with Cunningham Bus Services, Paisley. It displays the 'Blue Line' version of the livery. *(RM)*

Shown at the Town Hall and heading for Ulverston via Dalton on 24th April 1989 is East Lancashire-bodied Dodge 56 minibus No. 86. It is carrying the revised registration number which it received in December 1987 for reasons explained in the text. *(HP)*

Photographed in Ramsden Square on 19th May 1987 is Talbot minibus No. 89, heading for Ormsgill. These vehicles were leased and did not, therefore, pass to Ribble. *(HP)*

Northern Counties-bodied Leyland Atlantean No. 104 displays the BBT livery as it awaits departure from the Town Hall to Hawcoat on 27th December 1986. *(RD)*

RIBBLE'S SHORT REIGN

Ribble's reign in Barrow was shortly to end when this photograph was taken on 14th June 1989. Park Royal-bodied Leyland Atlantean No. 1399 is shown in Ramsden Square arriving from Ulverston. *(HP)*

Travelling along Abbey Road on Town Service B2 and heading for West Shore is Ribble Leyland National No. 426. *(HP)*

Eastern Coach Works-bodied Bristol LHS No. 271 approaches the Town Hall on 14th June 1989. It and sister vehicle No. 270 were previously allocated to Clitheroe depot and carried the name 'Betty's Bus' in honour of its regular lady driver. *(HP)*

Mercedes 608D minibuses were used to introduce Ribble's Town Service Network in Barrow and one of these, No. 518, is shown proceeding along Abbey Road towards the town centre. *(HP)*

Ribble originally brought in Talbot minibuses affording low-floor easy-access to compete with similar vehicles operated by Barrow Borough Transport Ltd. One of these, No. 070, has crossed the railway bridge in Abbey Road heading towards the town centre and South Walney. *(HP)*

Former Barrow Leyland National 1 No. 15 had been repainted into Stagecoach livery and carried Ribble fleetnames and fleet number 760 when photographed in Duke Street on 14th June 1989. *(HP)*

During Ribble's short reign, Cumberland loaned a number of Leyland Nationals to assist whilst former Barrow vehicles were being repainted. Included was No. 369 shown here at the Town Hall on service to West Shore. Note that the 'Cumberland' fleetnames had been removed for the period of the loan. *(HP)*

Ribble Leyland National 2 No. 857 passes through Ramsden Square *en route* to Newbarns. *(HP)*

CUMBERLAND IN BARROW

Former Barrow Leyland National No. 16 had been repainted and was displaying Cumberland fleetname and fleet No. 761 when photographed on 4th July 1989 travelling along Abbey Road and heading for West Shore. *(HP)*

Cumberland inherited the ex-Ribble Talbot minibuses and No. 078 was heading along Abbey Road on 4th July 1989. They retained Ribble livery and were withdrawn within a few months. *(HP)*

Although displaying Ribble fleetnames, Eastern Coach Works-bodied Leyland Atlantean No. 1415 was actually a Cumberland vehicle and displayed Cumberland legal lettering when photographed on Abbey Road on 4th July 1989. In order to assist standardisation, Park Royal-bodied Atlanteans which had previously operated in the area were replaced by Eastern Coach Works-bodied examples, similar to those which Cumberland had inherited from Ribble in Carlisle. *(HP)*

On 7th September 1989 former Barrow Leyland National No. 12 displays its new livery together with Cumberland fleetnames and fleet No. 757. *(HP)*

Photographed in Duke Street, approaching the Town Hall on 7th September 1989, is Leyland Lynx No. 251 on Service 2 to West Shore. *(HP)*

When photographed in Ramsden Square on 15th July 1992, Alexander-bodied Leyland Olympian No. 1090 was still carrying the registration number GSO 3V with which it had been re-registered by its previous owner, Bluebird Buses, from whom it had been purchased. It was further re-registered by Cumberland to reflect its true age and became C382 XAO. *(HP)*

Eastern Coach Works-bodied Leyland Olympian No. 2134 had formerly been in the Ribble fleet and was carrying 'Interlink' overall advertising livery when photographed in Duke Street on 15th July 1992 *en route* to Millom. *(HP)*

Former Ribble Mercedes 608D minibus No. 522 had been repainted and provided with Cumberland fleetnames when photographed in Duke Street on 7th September 1989. *(HP)*

Mercedes 608D minibus No. 44 was one of a number transferred from the Cumberland fleet to replace the Talbot minibuses which had been inherited from Ribble. It is shown at the Town Hall on 15th July 1992. *(HP)*

The Mercedes 709 minibus with Alexander coachbuilt body, as distinct from van conversion types, figured prominently in Stagecoach fleets. Cumberland No. 51 is shown in Duke Street on 15th July 1992 heading for Biggar Bank on service 1A. It was one of three which had been acquired from Hampshire Bus in 1989. *(HP)*

An internal view of the new depot showing a coach in the red 'Coachline' livery used by Cumberland for a while, also a minibus and National Expressliner No. 125 all receiving attention. *(HP)*

Leyland National B type No. 207 from the original Cumberland fleet was photographed at the Town Hall on 15th July 1992. *(HP)*

This metal cap badge is believed to have been part of the Corporation uniform but confirmation or any other information about this and any other badges worn would be appreciated, via the Publisher. *(GHC)*

A conductress displays the TIM ticket machine and heavy winter uniform. *(GHC)*

This conductress displays the lightweight jacket issued as part of the summer uniform. *(GHC)*

A conductor shows the standard male uniform, again with the TIM ticket machine. *(GHC)*

Bell Punch type tickets as used on trams with toll ticket for Walney Bridge.

Willebrew type return ticket as used on Coast Road services. The single ticket was white.

Bell Punch type tickets as used on early buses.

Bell Punch type ticket as used on the Ulverston service.

Ultimate type tickets. Values could be doubled by issuing two tickets together in tandem.

Willebrew type weekly ticket.

TIM roll ticket printed by ticket machine on white roll.

Setright roll ticket.

ABBEY ROAD (WEST), BARROW-IN-FURNESS

Hand-coloured postcards of street scenes were popular in most towns prior to the First World War, and, accordingly, often included trams in the scene. Above we see a tram on Abbey Road West, whilst below is another unidentified open-top tram arriving on Walney Island.

Park Royal-bodied Leyland PD2 No. 153,displays the blue and cream livery and the chassis/body combination so long associated with Barrow Corporation Transport. *(GL)*

Massey-bodied Leyland Tiger Cub No 53 dating from 1959 is shown at Ulverston awaiting the return journey to Barrow and seems to be carrying a good load of passengers. *(GL)*

An interesting scene in the town centre shows an East Lancashire-bodied Leyland Leopard L1 with Park Royal-bodied Leyland PD2s and at the extreme left a rear view of a Massey-bodied Leyland PD2. *(GL)*

Park Royal-bodied Leyland PD2 No. 170 delivered in 1958 is now preserved by John Hambler and attended the Open Day at Lillyhall depot in West Cumbria on 2nd June 2012, held to commemorate 100 years of Cumberland Motor Services. It is preserved in the earlier version of the blue and cream in which the batch was delivered. *(HP)*

Two vehicles from the batch of ten Park Royal-bodied Leyland PD2s delivered in 1958 are shown at the Town Hall in the later livery incorporating more cream. As mentioned elsewhere, No. 170 is now preserved in the earlier livery. *(AD)*

Photographed in the town centre in June 1977, with an East Lancashire-bodied Leyland Leopard L1 and the entrance to the market in the background, is Massey-bodied Leyland PD2 No. 108 in the later livery. *(AD)*

Leyland Leopards seem to abound in this photograph taken in June 1977. The example in the foreground, emerging from Duke Street into Schneider Square, is No. 68 with East Lancashire Coachbuilders body. *(AD)*.

Strachans-bodied Leyland Leopard No. 52 dating from 1966 was photographed on a sunny day in June 1977 near the Town Hall. *(AD)*

Neepsend-bodied Leyland Leopard No 56 dating from 1967 is shown in Ramsden Square still giving good service in July 1984. *(HP)*

East Lancashire-bodied Daimler Fleetline No. 5 is shown at Schneider Square heading for Tea House on 9th April 1983. *(RD)*

In summer sunshine on 22nd August 1984, Leyland National No. 6 has just crossed the railway bridge in Abbey Road as it heads into the town centre. *(HP)*

On 9th April 1983 East Lancashire-bodied Dennis Dominator No. 19 was standing at the Town Hall stop ready to depart to West Shore. Standing behind is a Leyland National 1 awaiting departure to Tea House. *(RD)*

Ex-London Transport Leyland Fleetline DMS No. 103 was carrying overall advert livery for Matthew Brown Lion Bitter as it proceeded down Abbey Road passing the railway station in August 1985. *(HP)*

Passing through Ramsden Square in July 1984 is Northern Counties-bodied Leyland Atlantean No. 105. *(HP)*

A view taken at the Town Hall shows Leyland Fleetline No. 103 in the Barrow Borough Transport Ltd livery but without the BBT fleetname which is clearly displayed on the unidentified wehicle parked behind. *(HP)*

When photographed in Abbey Road on 19th May 1987 Leyland Atlantean No. 104 was displaying the Barrow Borough Transport Ltd livery. This bus is now preserved. *(HP)*

Entering Duke Street from Ramsden Square on 24th April 1989 *en route* to West Shore is East Lancashire-bodied Dodge 56 minibus No. 85. **(HP)**

Parked at the Town Hall on 5th October 1988 is Talbot low-floor minibus No. 93 with a similar vehicle from the Ribble fleet parked behind. **(HP)**

Leyland National No. 16 had received the Barrow Borough Transport livery when photographed on 19th May 1987 loading for West Shore. *(HP)*

Duple Laser-bodied Leyland Tiger coach No. 80 displays the Barrovian Travel fleetname when parked at Blackpool in September 1986. *(MB)*

Former Barrow Leyland National No 13 was still in Barrow livery, but with Ribble fleetnames applied, when photographed in Poulton-le-Fylde as Ribble No 758. *(HP)*

Photographed on Fishergate Hill, Preston on 28th April 1993, is former Barrow Leyland Atlantean, No. 106. It is now displaying its new number, 1451, Ribble livery and fleetnames. *(RD)*

Photographed at the Civic Hall picking up passengers for Holbeck Farm in July 1989 is former Barrow Leyland National 2 No. 23 which had become No. 898 in the Cumberland fleet and was displaying Cumberland fleetnames. *(HP)*

Travelling along Abbey Road towards the town centre on service 6 from Ulverston is Alexander-bodied Volvo B10M No. 748. *(HP)*

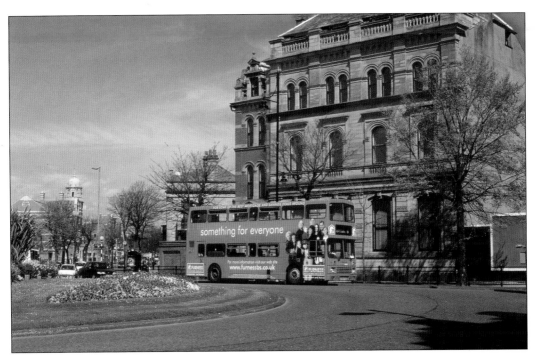

With Abbey Road in the background, Alexander-bodied Leyland Olympian No. 1003 is shown in Ramsden Square carrying overall advert livery for the Furness Building Society on 1st May 2001. It was the first in the first batch of these standard Stagecoach vehicles purchased by Cumberland in 1988 and numbered 1003-11 F803-11 FAO. They were originally used on Carlisle City Services. *(DMcA)*

Cumberland No. 1202 was one of two Alexander-bodied Leyland Olympian 96-seat 'Megadeckers' purchased in 1989. Originally they operated from Whitehaven depot but were later transferred to Barrow. It is shown in Ulverston, with the Hoad Monument in the background on 1st May 2001 operating on service 6. *(DMcA)*

Alexander-bodied Leyland Olympian No 14267 received Barrow Corporation livery and is shown in this livery in May 2008 on Windermere Road, Grange over Sands. It was operating on service X35 to Kendal presumably due to the none availability of a regular vehicle. *(HP)*

East Lancashire-bodied Dennis Trident No. 18280 displays the special livery for the X35 service as it enters the station forecourt at Grange over Sands in May 2008 on the return journey from Kendal to Barrow. *(HP)*

Optare Solo No. 47147 was painted in this special livery to mark the association of Barrow with the ship building industry over many years. It was photographed at the Open Day at Barrow Depot in May 2008. *(HP)*

Photographed in Cornwallis Street on 20th September 2010 is Optare Solo No. 47142 displaying the 'Network Barrow' sign at the side but not at the front. *(MB)*

Picking up passengers in Cornwallis Street, and illustrating the latest livery recently introduced for the Optare Solo vehicles, is No. 47136 on 21st November 2012. The 'Love Barrow' signage is visible. *(HP)*

Alexander-bodied Dennis trident No. 18140 was photographed on 27th September 2010 in Cornwallis Street awaiting departure to Ulverston on service 6. *(MB)*

Alexander-bodied Scania No. 15821 passes over the railway bridge on Abbey Road, Barrow as it arrives from Kendal on service X6 on 21st November 2012. *(HP)*

APPENDIX 1
BUS FLEET SUMMARY
BARROW IN FURNESS CORPORATION TRANSPORT

YEAR	REG. Nos.	FLEET No.	CHASSIS	BODY	SEATING	NOTES
1923	EO 3070		Ford	Allen	B14F	
1923	EO 3152/74	1/2	Chevrolet	MacPherson	B14F/12F	
1925	EO 3463	1	Guy B	Guy	B26F	
1925	EO 3482-5	2-5	Guy B	Guy	B26F	
1926	EO 3755-8	6-9	Guy B	Vickers	B26F	
1926	EO 3775-6	10/1	Guy JA	Guy	B14F	
1927	EO 4197/8	12/14	Guy BB	Guy	B26F	
1928	EO 4441/2	1/2	Guy B	Guy	B26F	
1929	EO 4678-81	15-8	Leyland TD1	Leyland	L24/26RO	
1931	EO 4998	7	Leyland TS3	Leyland	B32R	
1931	EO 5030/1	9/10	Leyland TS3	Leyland	B32R	
1931	EO 5162	19	Leyland TS3	Leyland	B32R	
1932	EO 5234-42	31-9	Crossley Condor	NCME	H24/24R	
1932	EO 5243-51	40-8	Crossley Condor	NCME	H24/24R	
1932	EO 5264	5	Crossley Alpha	Crossley	B32R	
1933	EO 5400-4	1-4/6	Leyland TS4	NCME	B32R	
1933	EO 5514/5	49/50	Crossley Condor	NCME	H24/24R	
1934	EO 5758/9	20/1	Leyland TD3c	NCME	H24/24R	
1935	EO 6065	22	Leyland TD4c	EEC	H24/24R	
1935	EO 6066	23	Crossley Condor	EEC	H26/22R	
1936	EO 6373-6	24-7	Leyland TD4c	EEC	H26/26R	
1937	EO 6634-7	11-4	Leyland TD4c	EEC	H26/26R	
1937	EO 6842	8	Leyland TD4c	EEC	H26/26R	
1937	EO 6843/86/87	28-30	Leyland TD4c	EEC	L26/26R	
1938	EO 7066-9	51-4	Leyland TD5c	EEC	L26/26R	
1938	EO 7141/2	55/6	Leyland TD5c	EEC	L26/26R	
1938	EO 7143-5	57-9	Leyland TD5c	EEC	H30/26R	
1938	EO 7146	60	Leyland TD5c	EEC	L26/26R	
1939	EO 7368-73	67-72	Leyland TD5c	EEC	H29/23R	
1939	EO 7520-5	62-6/ 61	Leyland TD5c	EEC	H29/23R	
1940	EO 7732-7	73-8	Leyland TD5c	EEC	H29/23R	
1941	EO 7802-5	15-8	Leyland TD7	East Lancs	H29/23R	
1942	EO 7859	79	Leyland TD7	East Lancs	H29/23R	
1942	EO 7882/3	80/1	Leyland TD7	Brush	H30/26R	
1942	EO 7893-6	82-5	Guy Arab I 5LW	Park Royal	H30/26R	
1942	EO 7901/2	86/7	Guy Arab I 5LW	Park Royal	H30/26R	
1943	EO 7904/5	91/2	Daimler CWG5	Massey	H30/26R	
1943	EO 7906-8	88-90	Guy Arab I 5LW	Massey	H30/26R	
1944	EO 7932	93	Guy Arab II 6LW	Massey	H30/26R	
1948	EO 8650-9	40-9	Crossley DD42/5	Crossley	H32/26R	
1948	EO 8788-97	101-10	Crossley DD42/4	Crossley	H32/26R	
1949	EO 8890-9001	111-22	Leyland PD2/3	Park Royal	H30/26R	
1949	EO 9050-67	123-40	Leyland PD2/3	Park Royal	H30/26R	
1950	EO 9171-80	141-50	Leyland PD2/3	Park Royal	H30/26R	
1951	EO 9502-9	151-8	Leyland PD2/3	Park Royal	H30/26R	
1951	EO 9510/1	159/60	Leyland PD2/3	Park Royal	H30/26RD	
1952	EO 9765/6	50/1	Leyland PSU1/13	Leyland	B44F	
1955	BEO 397	52	Leyland PSU1/13	Massey	B43F	

1958	CEO 948-57	161-70	Leyland PD2/40	Park Royal	H33/28R	
1959	EEO 468	53	Leyland PSUC1/1	Massey	DP39F	
1961	HEO 271-80	1-10	Leyland PD2A/27	Massey	H37/27F	
1963	JEO 768-73	68-73	Leyland L1	East Lancs	B42D	
1966	BEO 950-4D	50-4	Leyland PSU3/1R	Strachans	B51D	
1967	EEO 255-9E	55-9	Leyland PSU3/1R	Neepsend	B51D	
1968	GEO 160-4G	60-4	Leyland PSU3A/2R	East Lancs	B51D	
1969	HEO 245-9G	45-9	Leyland PSU3A/2R	East Lancs	B51D	
1971	LEO 141-5J	1-5	Daimler SRG6LX-36	East Lancs	B49D	
1971	BJH 128F	80	Bedford VAM70	Plaxton	C41F	
1973	ATF 740E	H1	Bedford VAL14	Duple Northern	C52F	h
1973	DTD 154E	H2	Bedford VAL14	Duple Northern	C52F	h
1973	KTC 361/2F	H3/4	Bedford VAL70	Duple Northern	C53F	h
1973	PTC 597/8G	H5/6	Bedford VAL70	Duple Northern	C53F	h
1973	VTJ 611/2H	H7/8	Bedford VAL70	Duple	C53F	h
1973	DTJ 632/3J	H9/10	Bedford VAL70	Duple	C53F	h
1974	SEO 206-8M	6-8	Leyland National	Leyland National	B49F	
1974	SEO 209/10M	9/10	Leyland National	Leyland National	DP48F	
1975	HEO 341-3N	H1-3	Bedford YRT	Duple	C53F	
1977	NEO 829-33R	11-5	Leyland National	Leyland National	B49F	
1978	UEO 478/9T	16/7	Leyland National	Leyland National	B49F	
1979	WEO 146/7T	18/9	Dennis Dominator	East Lancs	B46F	
1980	CEO 720-3W	20-3	Leyland National 2	Leyland National	B49F	
1982	OJD 174-6R	101-3	Leyland FE30AGR	MCW	H45/32F	I
1983	LEO 734-6Y	104-6	Leyland AN68D/1R	NCME	H43/32F	
1984	A266 PEO	107	Leyland AN68D/1R	NCME	H43/32F	
1984	OUC 41R	108	Leyland FE30AGR	MCCW	H43/32F	I
1984	OJD 227R	109	Leyland FE30AGR	MCCW	H43/32F	I
1986	C913 XEO	80	Leyland TRTCL11/3R	Duple Laser	C57F	
1986	CEO 952	81	Leyland PSU5A/4R	Duple Dominant	C53F	m

Notes :-

h) Ex-Hadwin Coaches

l) Ex-London Transport

m) Ex-Midland Red Coaches MWG 499P

APPENDIX 2
BUS FLEET SUMMARY
BARROW IN FURNESS BOROUGH TRANSPORT LIMITED

YEAR	REG Nos.	FLEET No.	CHASSIS	BODY	SEATING	NOTES
1986	LEO 141/2/4J	1/2/4	Daimler SRG6LX-36	East Lancs	B49D	a
1986	SEO 206-8M	6-8	Leyland 1151/1R	Leyland National	B49F	a
1986	SEO 209M	9	Leyland 11351/1R	Leyland National	B49F	a
1986	SEO 210M	10	Leyland 11351/1R	Leyland National	DP48F	a
1986	NEO 829-33R	11-5	Leyland 11351A/1R	Leyland National	B49F	a
1986	UEO 478/9T	16/7	Leyland 11351A/1R	Leyland National	B49F	a
1986	WEO 146/7T	18/9	Dennis Dominator	East Lancs	B46F	a
1986	CEO 720-3W	20-3	Leyland NL116L11/1R	Leyland National 2	B49F	a
1986	HEO 247-9G	47-9	Leyland PSU3A/2R	East Lancs	B51D	a
1986	EEO 256-9E	56-9	Leyland PSU3/1R	East Lancs	B51D	a
1986	GEO160-62/4G	60-2/4	Leyland PSU3A/2R	East Lancs	B51D	a
1986	C913 XEO	80	Leyland TRCTL11/3R	Duple Laser	C57F	a
1986	CEO 952	81	Leyland PSU5A/4R	Duple Dominant 1	C53F	a
1986	OJD 174-6R	101-3	Leyland FE30AAGR	MCW	H45/32F	a
1986	LEO 734-6Y	104-6	Leyland AN68D/1R	NCME	H43/32F	a
1986	A266 PEO	107	Leyland AN68D/1R	NCME	H43/32F	a
1986	OUC 41R	108	Leyland FE30AGR	MCW	H45/32F	a
1986	OJD 227R	109	Leyland FE30AGR	MCW	H45/32F	a
1986	D458/9 BEO	82/3	Dodge S56	East Lancs	DP22F	
1986	D460/56/7BEO	84-6	Dodge S56	East Lancs	B22F	
1987	E779 DEO	79	Dodge S56	Reebur	C25F	
1988	E657-9 OCW	76-8	Talbot Pullman	Talbot	B20F	
1988	E319/25 LHG	87/8	Talbot Pullman	Talbot	B20F	
1988	E327/32 LHG	89/90	Talbot Pullman	Talbot	B20F	
1988	E562-8 MAC	91-7	Talbot Pullman	Talbot	B20F	
1988	E569-71 MAC	98-100	Talbot Pullman	Talbot	B18F	
1989	GDR 205/6N	101/2	Leyland AN68/1R	Park Royal	H43/28D	p
1989	NXS 100L	103	Leyland AN68/1R	Alexander	H43/31F	d

Notes :-

a)Taken over from Barrow Corporation Transport

p)Ex-Plymouth City Transport

d)Ex-Delaine Ltd. Bourne

APPENDIX 3

BARROW IN FURNESS BOROUGH TRANSPORT LIMITED
VEHICLES TAKEN OVER BY RIBBLE MOTOR SERVICES LIMITED

BBT FLEET No	REG. Nos.	RIBBLE FLEET No	CHASSIS	BODY	SEATING	NOTES
82/3	D458/9 BEO	650/1	Dodge S56	East Lancs	DP22F	
84-6	D460/56/7 BEO	652/48/9	Dodge S56	East Lancs	B22F	
79	E779 DEO	653	Dodge S56	Reebur	C25F	
11-5	NEO 829-33R	756-60	Leyland 11351A/1R	Leyland National	B49F	
16/7	UEO 478/9T	761/2	Leyland 11351A/1R	Leyland National	B49F	
20	CEO 720W	895	Leyland NL116L11/1R	Leyland National 2	DP48F	
21-3	CEO 721-3W	896-8	Leyland NL116L11/1R	Leyland National 2	B49F	
104-6	LEO 734-6Y	1449-51	Leyland AN68D/1R	NCME	H43/32F	
107	A266 PEO	1452	Leyland AN68D/1R	NCME	H43/32F	
103	NXS 100L	1600	Leyland AN68/1R	Alexander	H43/31F	
101/2	GDR 205/6N	1653/4	Leyland AN68/1R	Park Royal	H43/28D	

APPENDIX 4
BUS FLEET SUMMARY
BRITISH ELECTRIC TRACTION CO. LTD. & BRITISH
AUTOMOBILE TRACTION CO. LTD.

YEAR	REG. Nos.	FLEET No.	CHASSIS	BODY	SEATING	NOTES
1914	EO 576		Daimler CD	?	B--	a
1914	EO 577		Daimler CD	Birch	B--	a
1914	EO 578		Daimler CD	Birch	Ch28	
1914	EO 579		Daimler CD	Birch	Ch28	
1914	EO 756		Daimler B	Brush	B26	a
1914	EO 757		Daimler B	Birch	B26	a
1915	EO 1052		Belsize 40HP	Birch	B--	
1915	EO 1053		Belsize 40HP	Birch	B--	
1915	EO 1054		Belsize 40HP	Birch	B--	
1920	EO 1054		Daimler CD	Birch	B--	b
1920	EO 2322		Daimler Y	Birch	B--	b
1920	EO 2323		Daimler Y	Birch	B--	b
1921	EO 2744		Daimler Y	Dodson	B26	b
1921	EO 2745		Daimler Y	Dodson	B--	b

Notes :-
a) Vehicles transferred from BET Ltd to BAT Ltd.
b) Vehicles new to BAT Ltd.

APPENDIX 5

BARROW IN FURNESS TRAMWAYS
ELECTRIC TRAM LIST

YEAR	CAR Nos	TYPE	BUILDER	TRUCKS	SEATING	NOTES
1903	1-7	Open-top	Brush	Brush A	22/26	g
1903	8-12	Single-deck combination	Brush	Brush B	36	g
1905	13/4	Demi-car	BEC	BEC Rigid Frame	22	g
1905	15/6	Open-top	Brush	Brush Conaty	28/32	g
1911	17-20	Open-top	Brush	Brill 22E	96	a,g
1913	21/2	Single-deck	Brush	Brush MET	40	g
1914	23/4	Single-deck	Brush	Brush MET	40	g
1915	25/6	Single-deck	Midland	Brill 22E	40	b,g
1917	27/8	Open-top trailer	Brush	Brush	18/30	c,g
1920	1-4	Single-deck combination	ER&TCW	Brill 21E	32	d,h
1920	29-34	Single-deck		Brill 21E	28	e,h
1921	35-46	Single-deck	Brush	Peckham P22	32	h

Livery :- BET - Maroon and Cream; Corporation - Olive Green and Cream

Notes
- a) Cars 19, 20 were converted to single-deck in 1928
- b) Built 1900 for Potteries Electric Traction Co. Series 71-85
- c) Trailers 27 & 28 were motorised after 1920, probably with trucks and equipment from 1-4
- d) Built 1900 for Southport Corporation. 2 & 3 became works cars at Barrow.
- e) Built for Sheffield Corporation Nos. 41 & 43 by Milnes in 1899. Nos. 100 & 102 by Brush in 1900 Nos. 126 & 206 by Sheffield Corporation in 1901 and 1902.
- g) Passed from BET Ltd to Barrow Corporation Tramways 1920
- h) New to Barrow Corporation Tramways

APPENDIX 6

STEAM TRAMS

Nos 1-8	Kitson & Co. 2 cylinder steam locomotive delivered July - August 1885
Nos 1-8	Falcon Engine and Car Works Trailer Car seating 30/28 delivered July - August 1885

In 1900 six Beyer-Peacock Wilkinson type steam tram engines were acquired from North Staffordshire Tramways Co. Ltd.

LIFE AFTER BARROW

A long way from Barrow. Former Barrow Strachans-bodied Leyland Leopard No. 51 crosses the bridge into Wadebridge, Cornwall on 25th September 1984. It was operating a School Service for its current owner Cornishman Coaches, Wadebridge. *(HP)*

Former London Transport Leyland Fleetlines Nos 101-3 were sold to Chester City Transport in 1988. No. 102 was numbered 75 by Chester and is shown in the city. *(AEJ)*

Two former Barrow vehicles which regularly attend the rally scene are CEO 957 seen at Heaton Park, Manchester, above and LEO 734Y (below) at The Trolleybus Museum at Sandtoft. *(JAS) (DC)*